# The Making of International Agreements

The Making of International Agreements

Congress Confronts the Executive

Loch K. Johnson

New York University Press
New York & London
1984

KF
5055
.J63
1984

Copyright © 1984 by New York University
All rights reserved
Manufactured in the United States of America

Library of Congress Cataloging in Publication Data
Johnson, Loch K., 1942–
  The making of international agreements.

  Bibliography: p.
  Includes index.
  1. Treaty-making power—United States. 2. United
States—Foreign relations—Executive agreements. 3. Executive power—United States. 4. Legislative power—United States 5. International obligations. 6. Diplomacy.
I. Title.
KF5055.J63 1984   342.73'06   84-1987
ISBN 0-8147-4165-7 (alk. paper) 347.3026

Clothbound editions of New York University Press books are Smyth-sewn and printed on permanent and durable acid-free paper.

Book design by Ken Venezio

*To my parents,
Kathleen and Roland Johnson,
with love and respect*

*and to the memory of Frank Church,
senator, philosopher, mentor, friend*

[The statesman's] instrument is diplomacy, the art of relating states to each other by agreement rather than by the exercise of force. . . .
—HENRY A. KISSINGER, *A World Restored*

The essence of government is power, and power, lodged as it must be in human hands, will ever be liable to abuse.
—JAMES MADISON

Contents

Figures	xi
Tables	xiii
Preface	xv
Acknowledgments	xix

I. **A Survey of International Agreements from the Cold War to Détente** — 1

   1. The Making of International Agreements — 3

   2. In Search of Friends: America's Agreement Partners — 31

   3. The Hidden Side of Agreement-Making — 56

II. **The Democratic Control of International Agreements** — 83

   4. The Bricker Revolt — 85

   5. A Second Resurgence — 116

   6. A Foreign Policy Partnership — 158

     Appendixes — 176

     Bibliography — 187

     Index — 201

Figures

1. International Agreement-Making: A Continuum of Executive Discretion — 7
2. Trends in the Content of U.S. International Agreements — 16
3. America's Major Agreement Partners: Twenty-Seven Countries Most Frequently Targeted for Bilateral Pacts (the Top Twenty Percent), 1946–73 — 37
4. Number of Significant Military Treaties and Executive Agreements — 62
5. U.S. House of Representatives, Committee on Foreign Affairs, Memorandum on International Agreements Submitted to Congress, October 1982 — 134
6. International Agreement Reporting Form (Case-Zablocki Act Input Format) — 166
7. Illustrative Codebook for the Reporting of International Agreements Under the Case-Zablocki Act — 168
8. A Systems Flowchart for the Monitoring of Reporting on International Agreements under the Case-Zablocki Act — 172

Tables

1. Form of U.S. Foreign Agreements by Administration, 1946–1972 — 13
2. Form of U.S. Foreign Agreements by Content Areas, 1946–1972 — 19
3. Form of U.S. Foreign Agreements by Content Area: The Truman Administration — 21
4. Form of U.S. Foreign Agreements by Content Area: The Eisenhower Administration — 21
5. Form of U.S. Foreign Agreements by Content Area: The Kennedy Administration — 22
6. Form of U.S. Foreign Agreements by Content Area: The Johnson Administration — 22
7. Form of U.S. Foreign Agreements by Content Area: The Nixon Administration — 23
8. Executive Agreement Index (EAI), 1946–1972 — 25
9. Regime Targets of U.S. Foreign Agreements by Administration, 1946–1972 — 34
10. Regime Targets of U.S. Bilateral Agreements by Five Policy Areas, 1946–1972 — 39

Tables

11. Regime Targets of U.S. Foreign Agreements by Form for Five Administrations, 1946–1972 — 41
12. Region Targets of U.S. Foreign Agreements by Administration, 1945–1972 — 45
13. Regional Priorities of U.S. Foreign Agreements by Content Area, 1946–1972 — 46
14. The Use of Three Forms of Agreement-Making Within Six Global Regions — 48
15. Most Favored Targets for U.S. Agreements, 1946–1972 — 50
16. Form and Content of U.S. Agreements with Most Favored Target Nations, 1946–1972 — 51
17. The Dominance of Executive Agreements over Treaties in the Making of Significant Military Commitments Abroad, 1946–1972 — 59
18. International Agreements (Other Than Treaties): A Frequency Distribution of Late Submissions to the U.S. Senate Committee on Foreign Relations, 1978 — 125
19. International Agreements Submitted to Congress by Executive Agencies, 1976 and 1977 — 129
20. A Comparison of Brickerites and Vietnam Insurgents by Party, Region, and Ideology — 146

Preface

The use of formal international agreements—that is, treaties, executive agreements, and statutory agreements—to bind the United States into relationships with other nations has long been an important instrument of American foreign policy. These agreements have frequently proved to be controversial and the question of agreement-making remains a subject of concern to public servants, attentive citizens, and students of international relations.

The idea for this volume grew out of the realization that, despite their importance, international agreements were dealt with in only the most superficial manner in books designed for college and university courses on international relations, international law, and American foreign policy. Typically, these books devote a few pages to the treaty-making process, a paragraph or two to executive agreements, and rarely anything at all to statutory agreements. Often only the question of treaties and how they are ratified is presented. As a consequence, the reader is left with little understanding of the complexities of international agreements, or the serious conflicts between the legislative and executive branches over how the different forms of agreements ought to be used.

Preface

What seemed to be missing was a book that would illustrate succinctly the types of international agreements used by the United States, the pattern of substantive commitments made by our country, the kinds of regimes that have attracted our negotiators, and the legal and political disputes that have resulted from the agreement-making process. Each of these topics needed to be examined over time to show the ebb and flow in the form and substance of agreements, as well as changing patterns in our ties with other countries.

The goals of this book, then, are to clarify the wide variety of techniques and objectives of formal diplomacy, and to explore the sharp disagreements among policymakers and scholars concerning the proper executive-legislative balance in the making of international agreements. The data, accumulated over a three-year period, reveal with detail and accuracy previously unavailable the array of formal agreements reached between the United States and other nations from 1946 to 1973—a period stretching from the early beginnings of the Cold War to the first stirrings of détente. This rich source of data, comprising over 6,000 agreements, is supplemented with extensive interviews conducted over the past decade with foreign policy practitioners in the executive and legislative branches.

Of course, American foreign policy is infinitely more complicated than the sum of various agreements signed with other nations. The great issues of war and peace, the extent of our moral obligation to help poor nations, the clash between Congress and the executive branch over constitutional prerogatives, the politics of regional alliances, the importance of psychological orientations held by decision-makers, and many other subjects make the study of foreign affairs endlessly fascinating and challenging. From this wide landscape, only a single portrait of American foreign policy is presented here: the formal and open commitments that have bound us abroad during the twenty-seven years following World War II and the tensions these commit-

Preface

ments have produced between Congress and the presidency. It is hoped that the statistical summaries and qualitative assessments of agreement-making offered in these pages shed light on this important dimension of American foreign policy.

This study is organized into six chapters. Chapter 1 acquaints the reader with the procedures of agreement-making. The three types or forms of formal agreements are defined and illustrated, and their frequency of use is traced over the years from 1946 to 1973. Following this discussion of the agreement form chosen by United States negotiators, the substantive content of the agreements is explored. The research has disclosed several major issue-areas into which international agreements may be grouped: military, economic policy and trade, communications, transportation, cultural-technical, and narrower diplomatic questions. Over the years, the interests of the United States have fluctuated with respect to these various areas; the first chapter presents the year-by-year priorities of American diplomacy as reflected in these fluctuations.

In chapter 2, the targets of American commitments overseas are examined. Specifically, the objective is to understand with whom the United States has felt most compatible over the years. The analysis focuses on three types of regimes (democratic, authoritarian, and totalitarian), six major regions (Latin America, Western Europe, Eastern Europe, Middle East, Africa, and Asia), and the key nations that have been our principal partners over the years. In terms of American alignments abroad, the research attempts to learn what nations have been our friends and what role the president and the Congress have played in choosing these friendships.

Chapter 3 departs from a statistical analysis to explore more qualitatively the question of agreement-making within, arguably, the most important issue-area: military policy. As a case study, this chapter points to an institutional disequilibrium in the making of commitments abroad—a dominance by the ex-

Preface

ecutive branch in the determination of military allies. In addition, the most elusive aspect of agreement-making is explored: informal agreements (based on verbal understandings—or misunderstandings) and secret agreements. International obligations are often consummated by the executive branch with little or no consultation, let alone debate, with the Congress or the American public. This chapter develops the thesis that, constitutional principles to the contrary, the executive branch has often proceeded secretly toward foreign commitments of great import on the assumption that Congress, presented with a fait accompli, would be compelled to honor the pledge.

Chapters 4 and 5 relate how the Congress has rebelled against freewheeling executive discretion in the making of international agreements, first through several unsuccessful bills advanced in the fifties (the Bricker Amendment movement), and then with a series of statutes passed in the seventies designed to restore the role of Congress (substantively as well as procedurally) in the establishment of American commitments abroad. These chapters further discuss various institutional and political problems associated with the democratic control of agreement-making.

Chapter 6 summarizes the normative theme of this volume: that foreign policy should be conducted on the basis of a partnership between the executive and legislative branches, and outlines some modest prescriptions toward this end with respect to agreement-making.

Lastly, this study offers an appendix and extensive bibliography. The appendix contains documents selected to give the reader a sense of primary sources in this field, and the bibliography identifies the most important studies published on the making of international agreements.

Acknowledgments

I am grateful to the many people who have helped with this project. I was provided vital financial assistance from the Ohio University Research Committee to support the initial data collection, and from the department of political science at the University of Georgia for computer time, clerical assistance, and travel support. I also had the good fortune to have several excellent research associates involved in the data-collection and coding phase of this study, notably Leena Johnson, Carol Gertner, Alison Jessen, Debbie Nellis, David Shambaugh, William P. Fong, Clai Rice, and Bob Bolin. I thank them for their painstaking care, and Joan Bowman, Kim Kelley, and Suzanne E. Overby for patiently typing drafts. I am pleased to thank, too, Samuel P. Huntington for editorial advice on an early segment of this research; Morton H. Halperin for sharing insights on military commitments abroad; the editors of *Foreign Policy*, *Journal of Politics*, and *Presidential Studies Quarterly* for permission to draw upon previously published work for portions of this study; Marjorie Ann Browne, Library of Congress, for access to her rich files and broad knowledge on agreement-making; Robert L. Chartrand, Library of Congress, for his advice

Acknowledgments

on congressional computer services; the staffs of the Senate Foreign Relations and House Foreign Affairs committees; the Department of State, Office of the Legal Adviser for Treaty Affairs, for responding quickly and courteously to several information requests; and, Colin Jones, Despina Papazoglou, and Sheila Rosensweig for their helpful editorial guidance. Last, but not least, I offer my sincere appreciation to Leena Johnson and John Lewis Gaddis for their encouragement along the way, and to James M. McCormick for his valuable recommendations at every stage of this project. Naturally, I alone am responsible for any errors that may appear in this work.

I.

A Survey of International Agreements from the Cold War to Détente

1.

The Making of International Agreements

> The constitutionally and historically sanctioned distinction between the treaty as the proper instrument for contracting important, substantive agreements and the executive agreement as an instrument for the conduct of routine and essentially nonpolitical business with foreign countries has now all but disappeared.
>
> —J. WILLIAM FULBRIGHT, *The Crippled Giant* (1972)

The Constitution of the United States envisages a partnership between the legislative and executive branches in the conduct of foreign policy. Among the shared powers is the prerogative to join in the establishment of commitments abroad, as expressed in the treaty-making provisions of Article II, Section 2 of the Constitution, the only explicit reference to international agreement-making in the founding document. This passage states that the president "shall have power, by and with the advice of the Senate to make treaties, provided two-thirds of the Senators present concur. . . ."

International Agreements from the Cold War to Détente

The role of the president and his subordinates in the executive branch has always been substantial in the making of treaties, reaching beyond the brief statement of Article II, Section 2. Hollis Barber has summarized the president's influence:

> It is on his initiative and responsibility that the treaty-making process is undertaken; he determines what provisions the United States wishes to have embodied in the treaty; he decides whether reservations or amendments that the Senate attaches to a draft treaty are acceptable to him and should be submitted to the other parties to the treaty; and, even if the Senate by two-thirds vote approves a treaty that he has negotiated, he may, influenced by change of heart or political conditions, decide not to ratify it and at the last minute file it in his wastebasket.[1]

The final ratification of a treaty, then, lies within the power of the president and not, as commonly misconceived, the Senate. He is the official who issues the formal statement indicating that the United States considers a treaty in effect and binding.

In spite of these considerable powers, however, the language of Article II, Section 2 is clear. As one legal scholar has put it, "The Founders made it unmistakably plain their intentions to withhold from the President the power to enter into treaties all by himself. . . ."[2] The Senate was meant to be a strong partner in the making of commitments overseas; yet in the modern era, presidents—and lesser members of the executive branch—have often involved this nation in significant foreign obligations without the advice and consent of the Senate or the counsel of the House. Designed to be the means to reach agreements with other nations, the number of treaties ratified has been few. Under a claim of constitutional prerogatives, frequently ill-defined, the executive branch has entered into many important international pacts merely with the stroke of a pen in hidden executive offices, far from the halls of Congress with its annoying habit of public debate.

The classic illustration comes from the administration of

The Making of International Agreements

Franklin D. Roosevelt. The president signed an agreement in 1940 with Great Britain (imperiled by an anticipated German invasion) to provide fifty aged United States destroyers in return for selected British naval bases in the Caribbean. Here was a broad commitment, providing the legal grounds for a German declaration of war against the United States. The treaty process, moreover, was bypassed: the president's signature sealed the pact. In this instance, the end result was undoubtedly worthwhile, but the method used had the effect of eroding the agreement-making procedure established by the Constitution. This solitary incursion on the Senate's treaty powers provided a precedent for further inroads, from military and economic commitments abroad to those dealing with transportation, communications, and several other policy areas.[3]

Awakened to the dangers of excessive presidential discretion during the Vietnam War era, critics pointed to the erosion of legislative participation in the making of international commitments. The criticism contended, first, that the *form* of international commitments had changed in recent years. Increasingly, the president used executive agreements, proclamations, or other unilateral instruments to circumvent the involvement of the Congress.[4] A second and related criticism centered on the *content* of the various international agreements. Even when the Congress was involved in the agreement-making process, the issues with which it dealt were substantively less important than those handled unilaterally by the executive. According to this view, for example, military agreements tended to take the form of executive agreements—thus excluding congressional participation—while economic or communication agreements (such as taxation agreements or radio regulations) were presented to the Congress in the form of treaties.[5]

Since the sixties, members of Congress have increasingly expressed frustration over the demise of the treaty procedure. While chairman of the Committee on Foreign Relations, Senator Fulbright complained: "The Senate is asked to convene solemnly to approve by a two-thirds vote a treaty to preserve cultural artifacts in a friendly neighboring country. At the same time, the chief executive is moving military men and material around the globe like so many pawns in a chess game."[6] His committee colleague Clifford Case (R, New Jersey) similarly observed: "We are not put in the Senate to deal only with treaties on copyrights, extradition, stamp collections and minor questions of protocol. If that is the meaning of the Constitution, then I think the Founding Fathers wasted their time."[7] With exasperation, the full Committee concluded in a 1969 report that: "We have come close to reversing the traditional distinction between the treaty as the instrument of a major commitment and the executive agreement as the instrument of a minor one."[8]

The problem is broadened further by yet more opaque forms of the executive agreement, including secret pacts whose existence are tightly held by the executive branch, verbal "promises" and "understandings" between nations—agreement-making by a smile and a wink—and agreements made by various bureaucratic officials, without the knowledge of the president or the Department of State (see figure 1).

In 1776, Thomas Jefferson urged: "On the subject of treaties, our system is to have none with any nation, as far as can be avoided."[9] Ironically, his wish has been practically granted; the treaty represents an all-but-discarded procedure.[10] Jefferson might be dismayed, however, by what has taken its place: international commitments based on loosely worded statutes and hidden transactions.

This chapter examines the validity of these criticisms by surveying systematically all nonclassified U.S. foreign policy commitments from 1946 to 1973.[11] Specifically, it seeks to determine the extent to which Congress and the executive branch have participated jointly in the making of international agree-

The Making of International Agreements

Figure 1
International Agreement-Making:
A Continuum of Executive Discretion

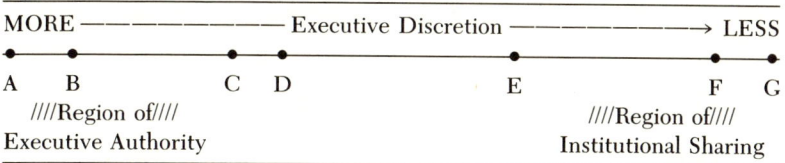

A. secret, verbal executive agreements ("understandings," "promises")
B. secret, written executive agreements (kept from Congress)
C. Secret verbal or written agreements (shared with select congressional committees)
D. Unclassified executive agreements
E. Statutory agreements
F. Agreements pursuant to treaties
G. Treaties

ments over that twenty-seven year period. It explores also the question of whether the involvement of Congress or the executive in agreement-making depends upon the content of the subject matter being negotiated. Are trivial matters left to the legislature while serious issues, like military policy, remain the special preserve of the executive? Finally, it evaluates the differences among five post–World War II presidencies (Truman through Nixon) regarding the form and content of international agreements made during their administrations. The chapter attempts especially to determine the extent to which the modern presidency has laid claim to constitutional authority in committing the U.S. abroad.

The research is organized in the following way. First, all international agreements between 1946 and 1973 that involved the United States were grouped according to form (executive agreements, treaties, or statutory agreements) and content (military policy, for example). The agreements were also coded as either bilateral (involving the United States and one other nation) or multilateral (involving the United States and at least two other nations or an international organization). The grouped data were then analyzed both in the aggregate and longitudinally as a means of assessing the pattern of executive and legislative relations in the making of international commitments.

Classifying International Agreements

Data for this study were compiled from various source materials on international agreements.[12] Some 6,015 agreements were signed and made public by the United States between January 1, 1946, and December 31, 1972.[13] These agreements were collected and coded according to form and content, using the following guidelines.

First, the form of each international commitment was determined on the basis of the legal authority claimed by the Department of State for signing each agreement. Combining the six categories established by the Department of State, Office of the Legal Adviser for Treaty Affairs, three basic forms were identified: agreements based in whole or in part upon the *authority and powers of the president* under the Constitution; agreements made pursuant to *congressional legislation;* and agreements approved by the *treaty process*, or made within the framework of treaty provisions without prior or subsequent legislation.[14] Thus, according to form, each agreement in this study was classified as an executive agreement (for example, base rights for Diego Garcia), a statutory agreement (economic assistance to another nation under PL-480) or a treaty (the North Atlantic Treaty of 1949). This classification roughly reflects a continuum of responsibility in agreement-making, ranging from "pure" executive authority in the form of an executive agreement to the most demanding form of institutional partnership in the form of a treaty.

Acceptance of the classification decisions reached by the Department of State poses some problems. As the Department of

The Making of International Agreements

State, Office of the Legal Adviser for Treaty Affairs, has noted, "Many of the agreements are difficult to fit into precise categories and opinions may differ as to the category in which a particular agreement should be placed."[15] The Department of State may have made judgmental errors that have been incorporated into this analysis. A potentially more serious concern is the possibility that the Department of State might have interpreted improperly, on some occasions, the basis of authority for various agreements, perhaps evenly broadly deriving statutory authority for agreements beyond the original intent of congressional legislation.

This is an important matter requiring a separate legal evaluation. This study does not attempt an assessment of the accuracy of the Department's classification decisions. They are amply documented, however, and await an assessment by legal scholars.[16] In the meanwhile, the Department of State opinions remain a particularly authoritative source regarding the degree to which various administrations have claimed constitutionally grounded executive authority for agreement-making. Preliminary comparison of the Department of State judgments with the actual language of the agreements strengthens one's confidence in its decisions.[17] Thus, it is believed that the data presented here provide a reliable perspective on the use of various froms of international agreements.

It should be emphasized again that those agreements classified as executive apply only to instances in which the president invoked constitutionally derived power to commit the United States abroad. Those agreements that are made by the executive pursuant only to congressional legislation are classified into the statutory category. While this distinction is generally recognized by scholars in the area, the tendency has been to place executive and statutory agreements under the same "executive agreement" (non-treaty) grouping.

Second, the content of the agreements was determined by

examining their subject matter. (For purposes of illustration, appendix A provides the text of a sample agreement.) While in each year international agreements cover a wide range of issues, the content areas are sufficiently the same that some general categories can be established. In 1972, for example, the United States signed agreements with other nations on the following topics (among many others):

>Television and radio facilities (Saudi Arabia)
>Trade: strawberries (Mexico)
>Satellite tracking station (Canada)
>Whaling: international observer scheme (Japan)
>Education program for agrarian reform (Philippines)
>Protection of migratory birds (Mexico)
>Atomic energy: cooperation for civil use (Japan)
>Military assistance (Malaysia)
>Air transport services (Czechoslovakia)
>Seabed arms control (multilateral)
>Cultural exchanges (USSR)
>Scientific and technical cooperation (USSR)
>Weather station (Honduras)
>Prevention of foot-and-mouth disease (Costa Rica)

These and other agreements signed by the United States were classified according to content in the following way:

>*Military.* Agreements on weapons systems; bases; military assistance, military alliances; training of military personnel; military supplies (such as naval vessels); arms control; and the like.
>*Economics and trade.* Agreements on commerce; agricultural commodities; trademarks; taxes on income and property; finance and debt rescheduling; economic assistance; fishing and whaling.

The Making of International Agreements

Transportation. Agreements on airlines and shipping; prevention of incidents on and over the high seas; tolls for international waterways; and the like.

Communication. Postal agreements; television and radio facilities; satellite telemetry and telecommand stations; and the like.

Health. Sanitation agreements; disease prevention; cooperation in medical science and public health; and the like.

Passports. Agreements on passports and visas; immigration quotas; free entry for diplomatic personnel; and the like.

Education. Agreements on educational exchanges and special educational programs.

Cultural-technical. Agreements on cultural exchanges; Peace Corps; scientific and technical cooperation; copyrights; tracking stations; environmental protection; energy (including atomic); protection of migratory animals; disaster assistance; weather stations; space cooperation; remote sensing for earth surveys; and the like.

Diplomatic recognition and relations. Agreements recognizing the existence of other nations; matters relating to foreign service personnel; international boundary disputes; exchange of official government publications; peace agreements; transfer of territory; and the like.

Claims. Agreements on repayment for expropriated property during time of peace.

War claims. Restitution of property seized during war; matters relating to military occupation; and the like.

For the analysis here, these separate categories were collapsed into the following broad groupings:

1. Military
2. Economics

International Agreements from the Cold War to Détente

3. Cultural-technical (including education and health)
4. Transporatation-communications
5. Diplomatic (including passports, claims and war claims)

Finally, it is important to note that each agreement was placed in only one category for the analysis.

Of course, not all of the thousands of agreements explored here are equal in rank. Some deal with the establishment of telephone or electrical service abroad, others with major defense commitments and atomic weapons. Comparisons based strictly on numbers obviously have their limitations. In these first two chapters, the focus is only on the frequency of the form and content of American commitments after World War II; in chapter 3, the research is extended into qualitative comparisons of agreements within the fields of defense and intelligence. In this way, the study tries to assay the quantitative and the qualitative dimensions of American commitments abroad.

The Form of International Agreements

The results of this analysis disclose that the overwhelming percentage—almost 87 percent—of all United States agreements between 1946 and 1973 have been statutory. By contrast, executive agreements and treaties account for only 7 percent and 6 percent, respectively, of all agreements during this period. These aggregate figures strongly suggest that Congress has been included in the agreement-making process; indeed, it has participated in the overwhelming percentage of them. At the same time, though, the data confirm the notion that the treaty has been replaced as the official instrument of foreign policy commitment. But again, in contrast to the conventional wisdom, treaties have been replaced not by executive agreements, but rather by statutory agreements—instruments involving both houses of Congress as well as the executive.

The Making of International Agreements

Table 1
Form of U.S. Foreign Agreements by Administration, 1946–1972

	Administration					
Form	Truman	Eisenhower	Kennedy	Johnson	Nixon	Average
Executive agreements	10.6%[a]	5.4%	3.8%	8.0%	9.1%	7.4%
Statutory agreements	79.5	89.2	92.7	86.7	86.4	86.7
Treaties	9.8	5.4	3.4	5.2	4.5	6.0
(N)	(1,315)	(1,884)	(783)	(1,143)	(866)	(5,991)[b]

[a] Entries are percentages based on column Ns shown at bottom. Some percentages do not add to 100 due to rounding error.

[b] Twenty-five agreements are excluded from this table and others where appropriate because they could not be classified by form.

When the use of the three forms was examined longitudinally, considerable stability in the pattern of use was found throughout this postwar period. Fluctuations have occurred only within relatively narrow ranges. Statutory agreements, for example, varied from 67 percent of all agreements in 1949 to 95 percent in 1962; treaties from 2 percent in 1962 to 15 percent in 1949; and executive agreements from 2 percent in 1961 to 20 percent in 1948. The dominant pattern across the years is for the statutory agreement to be used most often, the executive agreement second, and the treaty least of all. Such a pattern held in fifteen of the twenty-seven years, while in the other twelve years, the pattern was statutory agreement, treaty, and executive agreement. Even with the latter pattern, however, what was striking was the small gap in usage between treaties and executive agreements and the rather large gap between these two forms and the use of statutory agreements. The dominance of the statutory agreement, then, is evident: it has always been used most often as a method for formally committing the United States in foreign affairs during the post–World War II period examined here.

International Agreements from the Cold War to Détente

A similar conclusion emerged when the use of these different forms was examined by administration. The analysis failed to detect any dramatic differences among the five presidents (table 1). Each president (except President Truman) used the statutory agreement over 86 percent of the time for the formal conduct of American foreign policy. Even President Truman, who relied least upon this instrument, still used it 80 percent of the time. The major differences were that President Truman was most inclined to use executive agreements and President Kennedy the least inclined. The use of treaties has fallen off fairly steadily from the Truman administration through the Nixon administration.

In sum, the common argument that the form of international agreements has shifted from treaties to executive agreements, thereby excluding the Congress, fails to be supported by the evidence in this study. Moreover, when the data were examined from a number of different angles—over time, by administration, and by region—this conclusion remained unaltered. The next task was to explore whether certain international issues tended to be dealt with strictly or largely by executive agreements, excluding the Congress from active participation.

The Content of International Agreements

The time between World War II and the Vietnam War era was a period in American diplomatic history of active global involvement with other nations. Warmed by the heat of the Cold War, American alliances and commitments abroad spread rapidly throughout the noncommunist world between 1946 and 1973. In 1946, for example, the United States signed about one hundred international agreements; by 1972, the yearly volume of agreements had more than doubled. In 1946, the United States officially participated in 141 international conferences; by 1975, official American delegations traveled to over 800 conferences.

The Making of International Agreements

Increasing interdependence—a concept indicating mutual dependence among nations—aptly characterizes this era of American diplomacy.[18]

During this period, the predominant interest of the United States in the establishment of international agreements came in the area of economic policy and trade. About 37 percent of all agreements examined in this study were in this arena. The first Eisenhower term marked a dramatic turning point in our relations with other nations. In 1955, our pursuit of military defense pacts reached an apex; subsequently, American diplomatic activity focused increasingly (in terms of volume of commitments) on international trade agreements. This interest in economic interdependence reached a high point in the major efforts of the Kennedy administration to lower barriers and promote world trade in 1962. "The United States did not rise to greatness by waiting for others to lead. . . . Economic isolation and political leadership are wholly incompatible," said the President, and he introduced an unprecedented bill (the Trade Expansion Act of 1962) into the Congress, giving the White House a five-year authority to cut all tariffs by as much as 50 percent, as well as to slice to zero tariffs on those commodities traded chiefly by the United States and the Common Market.[19]

Overall, for four of the five administrations in this study, economic pacts were consistently greater in number than any other type of agreement. The exception was the Truman administration, in which cultural-technical agreements were most frequent. Furthermore, a yearly breakdown indicates that economic agreements (when compared to the other types of agreements) were most frequent in nineteen of the twenty-seven years. In particular, the Kennedy, Johnson, and Nixon administrations had the greatest percentage of agreements in the economic area (over 45 percent of each president's total), though the Eisenhower administration actually had the greatest number of such pacts, with some 625 economic agreements signed

International Agreements from the Cold War to Détente

during its longer tenure in office. (See figure 2 for a display of the various content areas by year.)

Interest in the enhancement of cultural-technical ties abroad

Figure 2
Trends in the Content of U.S. International Agreements

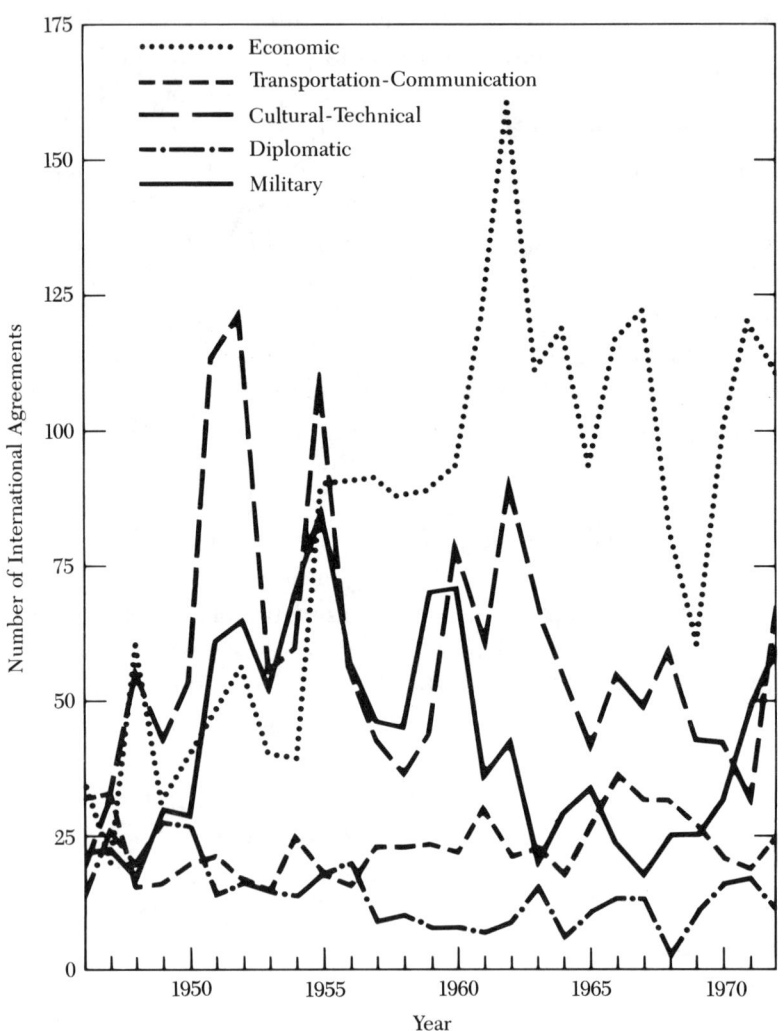

The Making of International Agreements

during the Truman years is attested to by the fact that 34 percent of his agreements were in this category. Such a percentage was higher than for any subsequent president and nearly surpassed the Eisenhower administration in total cultural-technical agreements (443 to 484), even though the latter was in office longer than Truman. Part of the reason is related to Truman's global political view. "I have been dreaming of TVAs in the Euphrates Valley to restore that country to the fertility and beauty of ancient times; of a TVA in the Yangtze Valley and the Danube," said President Truman to an associate.[20] His Point Four program was meant to be a step in this direction. One of Truman's White House advisers responsible for Point Four, Clark Clifford, believed that "it will be the judgment of history that— while Roosevelt created the New Deal in America—Truman extended it to the world."[21]

Though the enthusiasm in the Truman White House for the cultural-technical approach to interdependence was difficult to surpass, subsequent administrations have devoted considerable attention to such ties. In particular, the Kennedy administration signed nearly 27 percent of all its agreements in the cultural-technical area; the Johnson administration had 23 percent; and the Nixon administration completed just under 21 percent. For each of these three administrations, moreover, cultural-technical agreements surpassed military pacts in total frequency. Overall, then, economic and cultural-technical pacts have constituted almost 64 percent of America's international commitments from 1946 to 1973.

The third most frequent type of international agreement made by the United States during this period was the military pact. On average, these agreements constituted just over 19 percent of all commitments made by the United States abroad. The period of greatest expansion of these pacts took place during the Truman and Eisenhower years, as the Cold War intensified and the United States sought to contain communism through a se-

International Agreements from the Cold War to Détente

ries of security arrangements. President Truman agreed to some 257 military pacts (constituting 20 percent of all his commitments), while President Eisenhower completed almost 500 such agreements (constituting 26 percent of all his commitments). Later, military negotiations began to level out in the Kennedy and Johnson eras. For each of these two administrations, military ties consisted of only about 12 percent of all agreements, but an upward climb began once more under the next Republican president of the time span, Richard Nixon. During his first four years, he concluded some 162 military pacts and came close to rivaling Truman in the percentage of his commitments that were military (18 percent).

Finally, diplomatic issues (such as international boundary disputes and the establishment of diplomatic relations with other states), along with transportation and communication issues, have consistently drawn the least amount of attention for international agreement-making throughout the 1946–1972 period. On average, transportation and communication pacts constituted about 11 percent of all agreements; the Truman and Johnson administrations were most active in this area with 12 and 13 percent of all their agreements, respectively. The other administrations were all about 9 and 10 percent. The agreements in the diplomatic area comprised 6 percent of the total of all pacts. The Truman administration once again signed the greatest percentage of these ties (11 percent), and the Kennedy administration signed the least (4 percent). The other administrations had diplomatic pacts that constituted only 4 to 6 percent of their total international agreement-making.

In sum, the content of America's initiatives toward the world has been largely economic in nature, followed by a lesser (but persistent) interest in cultural-technical and military bonds, and lastly, a steady trickle of obligations dealing with transportation, communications, and diplomatic matters.

The Making of International Agreements

The Interplay of Form and Content

The use of the three major forms of agreements within each of the five content or issue-areas is presented in table 2. Statutory agreements are once again the dominant form, regardless of the content of the international agreement. Only in the case of diplomatic policy does the percentage of statutory agreements drop below 80 percent. The argument that the Congress has been systematically excluded from particular policy areas fails to be supported by these data. Differences across content areas do exist, however, for executive agreements and treaties. As table 2 illustrates, executive agreements have been used most frequently for military and diplomatic policy, and considerably less often for economic, transportation-communication, and cultural-technical policies. In contrast, treaties have been used most frequently for diplomatic and transportation-communication policy, less often for economic policy, and least of all for military and cultural-technical policy.

In comparing policy differences within each form, then, these results lend some credence to the proposition that vital issues like military commitments have sometimes been handled through

Table 2
Form of U.S. Foreign Agreements by Content Areas, 1946–1972

	Content				
Form	Military	Economic	Transportation-Communication	Cultural-Technical	Diplomatic
Executive agreements	12.4%[a]	4.6%	5.9%	3.7%	26.7%
Statutory agreements	84.0	88.6	84.6	93.2	60.1
Treaties	3.6	6.8	9.5	3.2	13.2
(N)	(1,146)	(2,229)	(630)	(1,580)	(371)

[a] Entries are percentages based on column Ns shown at the bottom. Thirty-five agreements, representing 0.6% of the total, were classified as "Other" for content and are not shown in the table.

a form removed from congressional participation. Seemingly less critical matters, however, such as cultural-technical, economic, and transportation-communication policy, have been dealt with in a way that allowed congressional action. While the proposition thus has some accuracy, it should not be exaggerated in light of the large number of statutory agreements across all policy areas. If we were to assume that all secret executive agreements (perhaps as high as an additional 10 percent of the total) were military, the total percentage of military executive agreements would still not be much higher than 30 percent. Such a percentage would reinforce the argument about military policy being more subject to executive discretion, but it would not alter the basic finding regarding the dominance of the statutory agreement, even in this policy arena. The question of executive discretion in military policy will be examined in greater detail in chapter 3.

Presidential Patterns

Have the five presidencies studies here differed significantly in the form and content of agreements signed during each administration? Especially, to what extent have presidents differed in their use of executive agreements for all content areas? When the form and content of agreements were examined for each of the five administrations, little difference was found from the aggregate conclusion presented earlier.[22] Tables 3 through 7 portray the results for each president.

In each administration, the statutory pact dominated the agreement-making process. Rarely did the percentage of statutory agreements fall below 80 percent in any policy area. The exception for all five administrations came in the area of diplomatic policy, where the presidents averaged just over 50 percent. Moreover, the Kennedy and Johnson administrations had only 41 percent and 47 percent, respectively, in this category.

The Making of International Agreements

Table 3
Form of U.S. Foreign Agreements by Content Area:
The Truman Administration

	Content				
Form	Military	Economic	Transportation-Communication	Cultural-Technical	Diplomatic
Executive agreements	16.7%[a]	14.2%	4.4%	1.8%	27.1%
Statutory agreements	75.4	65.9	82.5	95.3	62.5
Treaties	8.1	19.9	13.1	2.9	10.4
(N)	(257)	(296)	(160)	(443)	(144)

[a] Entries are percentages based on column Ns shown at bottom. Fifteen agreements, representing 1.1% of the total, were classified as "Other" for content and are not shown in the table.

Only two administrations—Truman's and Johnson's—had statutory agreement levels below 80 percent in any other content arena. President Truman fell below this figure for military pacts (75 percent) and for economic agreements (66 percent), and President Johnson fell below for military pacts (70 percent).

With respect to treaties, four of the administrations used this

Table 4
Form of U.S. Foreign Agreements by Content Area:
The Eisenhower Administration

	Content				
Form	Military	Economic	Transportation-Communication	Cultural-Technical	Diplomatic
Executive agreements	8.5%[a]	1.1%	6.6%	2.5%	27.9%
Statutory agreements	89.9	90.6	83.1	95.5	60.6
Treaties	1.6	8.3	10.2	2.1	11.5
(N)	(497)	(625)	(166)	(484)	(104)

[a] Entries are percentages based on column Ns shown at bottom. Eight agreements, representing 0.4% of the total, were classified as "Other" for content and are not shown in the table.

International Agreements from the Cold War to Détente

Table 5
Form of U.S. Foreign Agreements by Content Area:
The Kennedy Administration

	Content				
Form	Military	Economic	Transportation-Communication	Cultural-Technical	Diplomatic
Executive agreements	5.3%[a]	1.1%	8.6%	3.8%	24.1%
Statutory agreements	93.7	96.0	90.0	94.3	41.4
Treaties	1.1	2.9	1.4	1.9	34.5
(N)	(95)	(378)	(70)	(210)	(29)

[a] Entries are percentages based on column Ns shown at bottom. One agreement, representing 0.1% of the total, was classified as "Other" for content and is not shown in the table.

form most frequently for diplomatic commitments. (President Truman used the treaty form most frequently for economic ties.) In the other policy areas, the treaty form varied in usage by the five administrations, but it is striking how infrequently this approach was used for military ties. For three of the administrations (Eisenhower, Kennedy, and Johnson), the military area had the lowest percentage of treaties, while for the other two ad-

Table 6
Form of U.S. Foreign Agreements by Content Area:
The Johnson Administration

	Content				
Form	Military	Economic	Transportation-Communication	Cultural-Technical	Diplomatic
Executive agreements	25.9%[a]	4.2%	3.4%	4.2%	37.8%
Statutory agreements	70.4	91.9	87.2	90.9	46.7
Treaties	3.7	3.8	9.5	4.9	15.6
(N)	(135)	(546)	(148)	(263)	(45)

[a] Entries are percentages based on column Ns shown at bottom. Six agreements, representing 0.5% of the total, were classified as "Other" for content and are not shown in the table.

The Making of International Agreements

Table 7
Form of U.S. Foreign Agreements by Content Area:
The Nixon Administration

	Content				
Form	Military	Economic	Transportation-Communication	Cultural-Technical	Diplomatic
Executive agreements	10.5%[a]	7.0%	9.3%	10.6%	14.3
Statutory agreements	85.8	90.9	82.6	83.9	75.5
Treaties	3.7	2.1	8.1	5.6	10.2
(N)	(162)	(384)	(86)	(180)	(49)

[a] Entries are percentages based on column Ns shown at bottom. Five agreements, representing 0.6% of the total, were classified as "Other" for content and are not shown in the table.

ministrations (Truman and Nixon) it had the second lowest. Military agreements seem rarely to assume the treaty form.

By contrast, note the extensive use of the executive agreement for both military and diplomatic policy by the various administrations. With the exception of President Kennedy, all the chief executives have used executive agreements to a much greater extent for military and diplomatic affairs than for the other major policy areas. Presidents Truman and Johnson had the highest percentages of executive agreements for military pacts (17 percent and 26 percent, respectively), with Presidents Eisenhower and Nixon (9 percent and 11 percent) close behind. In the diplomatic area, the percentage of executive agreements used by each of the administrations was generally much higher; four of the presidents (Truman, Eisenhower, Kennedy, and Johnson) used executive agreements around 25 to 38 percent in this policy area.

To explore more fully, and from a different angle, the use of executive discretion in foreign affairs among the five postwar presidents, a simple Executive Agreement Index (EAI) was constructed for each administration. The index is based upon the proportion of executive agreements (EA) among the total number of treaties (T) and executive agreements: EA/(T + EA). (See table 8.) This index provides an indication of the degree of activism in foreign affairs for each president. The use of treaties and executive agreements was compared, since they have been far more controversial than statutory agreements.

The data in table 8 show that, across the board, President Nixon was the most robust in the rejection of the treaty procedure. He was more apt than any of the other presidents to claim Constitutional authority as chief executive to commit the United States abroad. Perhaps this should fail to surprise, since certainly none of the other presidents on this list ever described the powers of the presidency so expansively as did President Nixon in retirement. In response to a Senate committee interrogatory concerning the right of presidents to violate the law to protect national security, the former president replied:

It is quite obvious that there are certain inherently governmental actions which if undertaken by the sovereign in protection of the interest of the nation's security are lawful but which if undertaken by private persons are not. . . . [I]t is naive to attempt to categorize activities a president might authorize as "legal" or "illegal" without reference to the circumstances under which he concludes that the activity is necessary. Assassination of a foreign leader—an act I never had cause to consider and which under most circumstances would be abhorrent to any president—might have been less abhorrent and, in fact, justified during World War II as a means of preventing further Nazi atrocities and ending the slaughter. Additionally, the opening of mail sent to selected priority targets of foreign intelligence, although impinging upon individual freedom, may nevertheless serve a salutary purpose when—as it has in the past—it results in preventing the disclosure of sensitive military and state secrets to the enemies of this country.

In short, there have been—and will be in the future—circumstances in which presidents may lawfully authorize actions in the interests of the security of this country, which if undertaken by other persons, or even by the president under different circumstances, would be illegal.[23]

The Making of International Agreements

While President Nixon thus scored highest in the use of executive agreements over treaties, a general increase in the exercise of executive discretion is evident in the trends. Although this discretion did not increase uniformly over time, the pattern is unmistakable: presidents have relied more and more on the executive agreement at the expense of the treaty in the international agreement process.

The military policy area has been the most susceptible to this executive discretion, although President Nixon tended to use less unilateral authority here than did Presidents Johnson, Eisenhower, or Kennedy. For Presidents Eisenhower and Johnson, the EAI for military matters surpassed that for all policy areas. Even with the other three presidents, the military EAI ranked second. Furthermore, there appeared to be a similar trend of increased executive discretion over the five administrations in the economic area, too, reaching an EAI of .77 for President Nixon. A comparable pattern, albeit less clear-cut, has occurred in the cultural-technical area, with Presidents Nixon

Table 8
Executive Agreement Index (EAI), 1946–1972 [a]

	Policy Area [b]					
Administration	Military	Economic	Transportation-Communication	Cultural-Technical	Diplomatic	Average
Truman [c]	.67	.42	.25	.38	.72	.49
Eisenhower	.84	.12	.39	.55	.71	.52
Kennedy	.83	.27	.86	.67	.41	.61
Johnson	.88	.52	.26	.46	.71	.57
Nixon [d]	.74	.77	.53	.66	.58	.66
Average	.79	.42	.46	.54	.63	

[a] This table summarizes the use of military treaties and executive agreements only; statutory agreements, which are more numerous but less controversial, are not analyzed here.

[b] The numbers in each column represent for each administration the proportion of executive agreements compared to the total number of treaties and executive agreements EA/(T + EA). This Executive Agreement Index ranges from 0 to 1; the higher the index, the greater the reliance on executive agreements for commitments abroad.

[c] Data are for 1946–1952.

[d] Data are for 1969–1973.

International Agreements from the Cold War to Détente

and Kennedy reaching .66 and .67 on the index. Finally, and conversely, the diplomatic policy area, while quite high in overall executive discretion, has shown some signs of moderating over the twenty-seven-year period of this study.

A Recapitulation

Two major trends characterize the data analysis in chapter 1: the importance of the statutory agreement as the major formal instrument of American commitments abroad, and the accelerated use of the executive agreement—despite the prominence of the statutory agreement—as an important vehicle for military and diplomatic commitments.

The first result implies a greater *procedural* involvement in the agreement-making process than conventional wisdom suggests. Despite such a procedural role, however, one cannot conclude necessarily that the Congress plays a large *substantive* role. Instead, the findings suggest only that members of Congress have been asked to give and have given an official green light to the vast majority of overseas commitments—most initiated by the executive branch. Whether or not the Congress always knew precisely what it approved, though, is quite a different question. In fact, earlier studies,[24] as well as the author's own interviews and observations, suggest that the legislative branch is often deficient in the substantive area—the meaningful details of policy—despite its considerable procedural involvement in the approval of international commitments.

The second major finding implies that presidential discretion over selected issues has been substantial in the postwar period. While this discretion has been confined primarily to military and diplomatic matters, the commitment of armed force is of course of great importance for American foreign policy. In an attempt to understand more thoroughly the significance of this discretion in the military area, in chapter 3 those executive agree-

The Making of International Agreements

ments and treaties of a military nature are examined. First, though, this survey of the agreement-making process is completed by examining the targets of American commitments during the period from 1946 to 1973.

Notes

1. Hollis W. Barber, *Foreign Policies of the United States* (New York: Dryden, 1953), p. 30.
2. Raoul Berger, "The Presidential Monopoly of Foreign Relations," *Michigan Law Review* 71 (1972), p. 39.
3. This instance was not the first time in which the executive agreement was used to make commitments with other nations. For examples of the executive agreements used earlier in the history of the country, see Arthur M. Schlesinger, Jr., "Congress and the Making of American Foreign Policy," *Foreign Affairs* 51 (October 1972), pp. 78–113; and Louis Fisher, *The President and Congress: Power and Policy* (New York: Free Press, 1972).
4. Among many who make this argument are Louis Fisher, *The President and Congress: Power and Policy*, pp. 42–47; Arthur M. Schlesinger, Jr., *The Imperial Presidency* (New York: Houghton Mifflin, 1973), pp. 310–319; J. William Fulbright, *The Crippled Giant* (New York: Random House, 1972), pp. 216–227; James A. Robinson, *Congress and Foreign Policy Making: A Study in Legislative Influence and Initiative*, rev. ed. (Homewood, Illinois: The Dorsey Press, 1967); and Stan A. Taylor, "Congressional Resurgence," in ed. Martin B. Hickman, *Problems of American Foreign Policy*, 2nd ed. (Beverly Hills: Glencoe Press, 1975), pp. 106–118.

One of the first modern legislators to sound an alarm over the use of executive agreements was John Bricker (R, Ohio), who led an effort in the Senate during the fifties to trim President Eisenhower's agreement-making powers. The so-called Bricker Amendment (Senate Joint Resolution 1), examined in chapter 4, failed by a single vote. For an early and eloquent expression of concern over the erosion of the treaty power voiced by a senator during the Vietnam War era, see Frank Church (D, Idaho), "Of Presidents and Caesars: The Decline of Constitutional Government in the Conduct of American Foreign Policy," *Idaho Law Review* 6 (Fall 1969), pp. 1–15.

For other discussions on executive-congressional relations in foreign policymaking, see Robert A. Dahl, *Congress and Foreign Policy* (New York: Harcourt, Brace, 1950); Ronald C. Moe and Steven C. Teel, "Congress as Policy Maker: A Necessary Reappraisal," in Douglas M. Fox, ed., *The Politics of U.S. Foreign Policy Making* (Pacific Palisades, California: Goodyear Publishing Company, 1971), pp. 157–160; Amy M. Gilbert, *Executive Agreements and Treaties, 1946–1973* (Endicott, New York: Thomas-Newell, 1973); and

International Agreements from the Cold War to Détente

Louis Henkin, *Foreign Affairs and the Constitution* (Mineola, New York: Foundation Press, 1972), which has an especially good discussion of the treaty process on pp. 129–171. Two recent books are Thomas M. Franck and Edward Weisband, *Foreign Policy by Congress* (New York: Oxford, 1979), and Cecil V. Crabb, Jr. and Pat Holt, *Invitation to Struggle: Congress, the President and Foreign Policy* (Washington, D.C.: Congressional Quarterly Press, 1980). Two recent articles are John G. Tower, "Congress Versus the President: The Formulation and Implementation of American Foreign Policy," *Foreign Affairs* 60 (Winter 1981/1982), pp. 229–246, and Warren Christopher, "Ceasefire Between the Branches: A Compact in Foreign Affairs," *Foreign Affairs* 60 (Summer 1982), pp. 989–1005. A more exhaustive listing is provided in the bibliography.

5. The reference is a paraphrase of Senator J. William Fulbright's (D, Arkansas) comments in his *The Crippled Giant*, in which he contrasted the content of treaties and executive agreements for 1954 and 1968.

6. Subcommittee on Separation of Powers, Senate Judiciary Committee, "Congressional Oversight of Executive Agreements," *Hearing*, 92nd Cong., 2nd Sess. (1972), p. 249.

7. Cited by Arthur M. Schlesinger, Jr. in *The Imperial Presidency*, p. 313.

8. "National Commitments," Senate Report 91–129, 91st Cong. 1st Sess., April 16, 1969, p. 28.

9. Cited by Henkin, p. 372.

10. Significant recent exceptions include the Strategic Arms Limitations Talks, SALT I, treaty (ABM Treaty) of 1972, the Panama Canal Treaties (1978), and the SALT II treaty, proposed in 1979 but subsequently withdrawn from the Senate.

11. Classified agreements obviously are not included in this analysis. A senior staff member of House Foreign Affairs Committee estimated that from 5 to 10 percent of all international commitments are secret and mainly deal with military policy (interview, June, 1974, Washington, D.C.). Since no systematic record exists of the various verbal agreements between the United States and other nations, this analysis excludes these informal understandings. (See chapter 3 for further discussion of secret and informal agreements.)

12. The following sources were used: *United States Statutes At Large*, which lists treaties and other international agreements entered into prior to 1950; *United States Treaties and Other International Agreements*, which covers agreements entered into force on or after January 1, 1950; *Treaties and Other International Acts Series*, numbered pamphlet copies of international agreements; and *Digest of United States Practice in International Law*. Each of these documents is published by the Government Printing Office, Washington, D.C.

13. The signing of an international agreement does not always bring it into force. Instead, the signing may be only a preliminary act. For example, a treaty

The Making of International Agreements

may be signed but never ratified; that is, it may never come to bind the parties. The date of initial signing, however, is used in this analysis, rather than the date of effectiveness, since the focus here is primarily on the initiation of the commitment by the executive and the Congress.

These data are essentially the same as the data analyzed in earlier articles: Loch Johnson and James M. McCormick, "The Making of International Agreements: A Reappraisal of Congressional Involvement," *The Journal of Politics* 40 (May 1978), pp. 468–478; "Foreign Policy by Executive Fiat," *Foreign Policy* 28 (Fall 1977), pp. 117–138; and "The Democratic Control of International Commitments," *Presidential Studies Quarterly* 8 (Summer 1978), pp. 275–308). Further scrubbing and tightening of the data took place in the preparation of this volume and accounts for modifications in the tables. The general conclusions remain essentially the same. These years were analyzed because they mark the limits of the Cold War period (or at least Cold War I). With the signing of several military, economic, and cultural pacts with the Soviet Union in May 1972, the Nixon administration launched its policy of détente, an effort to ease the acrimony during the previous three decades of the Cold War.

14. The data source for this classification of the agreements was *International Agreements Other than Treaties, 1946–1968: a List with Citation of Their Legal Basis*, Department of State, Office of the Legal Adviser for Treaty Affairs, January 10, 1969, mimeographed, supplemented with updating addenda. In addition, telephone interviews with this Office were used to assist in the classification of some agreements. Twenty-five agreements had to be excluded from the analysis of form because Deparment of State classifications were unavailable.

No doubt the listings in *Treaty and Other International Agreements* fail to reflect all international agreements. David J. Kuchenbecker reports, for instance: "Former Secretary of State John F. Dulles estimated in 1953 that some 10,000 executive agreements have been made under the treaty [the NATO treaty]." See his "Agency-Level Executive Agreements: A New Era in U.S. Treaty Practice," *Columbia Journal of International Law* 18 (1979), p. 30, footnote 103. Moreover, the 1979 SALT II agreement was never officially recognized, since it was only informally honored by both parties as they awaited a treaty review. The data here, then, do not capture the entire universe of American commitments abroad. They do capture those officially recognized agreements, though, which include most of the important ones.

15. *International Agreements Other than Treaties, 1946–1968*, p. iii.
16. Ibid.
17. Before discovering the State Department classification cited in note 14 above, the agreements were coded in a preliminary fashion according to the legal citations in the text of each agreement. For example, when legislation was cited as the basis for the agreement, the pact was coded as statutory un-

less the legislation was in the form of a treaty or pursuant to a treaty. In that case, it was coded as a treaty. All agreements without legal citations were coded as executive agreements. Preliminary analyses with these data compared quite favorably with the classification developed by the Department of State. As a result, it was decided to use the Department's criteria for classifying all agreements.

18. See Joseph S. Nye, "Independence and Interdependence," *Foreign Policy* 22 (Spring 1976), p. 145.

19. Quoted in Theodore C. Sorenson, *Kennedy* (New York: Harper, 1965), p. 411.

20. Quoted in Alonzo L. Hamby, *Beyond the New Deal: Harry S. Truman and American Liberalism* (New York: Columbia, 1973), p. 371.

21. Ibid., p. 372.

22. The period of each administration was defined as follows for the data analysis: President Truman, January 1, 1946 to January 20, 1953; President Eisenhower, January 21, 1953 to January 20, 1961; President Kennedy, January 21, 1961 to November 22, 1963; President Johnson, November 23, 1963 to January 20, 1969; President Nixon, January 21, 1969 to December 31, 1972.

Calendar years were used for each administration in earlier publications using this data; therefore, this recording produces slight differences in the results.

23. "Supplementary Detailed Staff Reports on Foreign and Military Intelligence," appendix, book IV, *Final Report of the Select Committee to Study Governmental Operations with Respect to Intelligence Activities* (the Church Committee), Report No. 94–755, U.S. Senate, 94th Cong., 2nd Sess., April 23, 1976, pp. 157–158.

24. See, for example, Theodore J. Lowi, *The End of Liberalism*, 2nd ed. (New York: W. W. Norton, 1979).

2.

In Search of Friends: America's Agreement Partners

> When they had once got it by heart, the sheep developed a great liking for this maxim, and often as they lay in the field they would all start bleating "Four legs good, two legs bad! Four legs good, two legs bad!" and keep it up for hours on end, never growing tired of it.
>
> —GEORGE ORWELL, *Animal Farm*

Agreement Targets

In chapter 1, the role of the Congress and the president in the agreement-making process was examined according to the form and content of these pacts. In this chapter, the analysis is taken a step further by exploring the selection of agreement partners made by the United States. The aim here is to assess the extent to which our country has initiated pacts with particular states, regions, and regimes. More precisely, the central questions asked are: (1) What kinds of regimes (totalitarian, authoritarian, or democratic) have been the principal partners of the United States for its international agreements? (2) What has

International Agreements from the Cold War to Détente

been the relative importance of particular regions for American diplomats? (3) What specific nations have attracted the most commitments from the United States over time? Throughout this survey, a major focus is on the relative role of the Congress and the president in completing agreements with different regimes, regions, and nations. Normatively, the record indicates a propensity in American foreign policy to stereotype (in a way reminiscent of Orwell's sheep) rightist regimes as good and leftist regimes as bad.

Regimes and Foreign Policy Commitments

Initially the analysis examines the types of nations with which the United States has made commitments over the era covered by this data. Much has been said about America's ties with individual authoritarian or totalitarian regimes, but few studies have surveyed a wide range of international commitments to achieve a more accurate portrait of United States policy abroad. Such evidence enhances the opportunity for an informed discussion of American commitments abroad—including the inescapable normative issues.

This analysis concentrates on bilateral agreements and classifies all those nations that were targets of American commitments into one of three categories: democratic, authoritarian, or totalitarian. Democratic regimes are conceptualized as states where parties or groups compete for office in relatively free elections; authoritarian, or anticommunist "right-wing" regimes, as states where political power is in the hands of a single ruler, the military, or a civilian oligarchy without the benefit of free elections; and totalitarian, or communist "left-wing" regimes, as states where the Communist party or a Marxist group holds the preponderance of political power within the society.[1]

To develop this typology, other regime classifications were first consulted. Particularly helpful were Arthur Banks's *Politi-*

In Search of Friends: America's Agreement Partners

cal *Handbook of the World* and the Central Intelligence Agency's *National Basic Intelligence Factbook*.[2] These two sources provide an academic and an official government assessment of regime types. The typology here was constructed by blending these sources with personal judgments and the advice of area specialists in the author's academic department. By this process, a year-by-year classification emerged. Consultations with area specialists in the Department of State and on Capitol Hill provided further information for this classification process. As the typology is limited to three categories, less likelihood of distortion exists than if it had been composed of a higher degree of classification. Moreover, the typology possesses considerable face validity; those nations one commonly thinks of as democracies are indeed democracies in the typology, as is the case for authoritarian and totalitarian regimes.

An Affinity for Democracies

The analysis disclosed that 3,071, or 58 percent, of all international bilateral agreements signed by the United States during the Cold War were with democratic regimes; 2,011, or 38 percent, with authoritarian regimes; and a modest 247, or 5 percent, with totalitarian regimes (see table 9).[3] Moreover, this ranking of agreement partners generally held across the five administrations during the Cold War (though the Nixon administration signed as many agreements with authoritarian regimes as with democracies).

Despite such consistency in ranking, some important fluctuations occurred in the relative percentage of agreements with each kind of regime.[4] A substantial decline occurred in ties with other democracies, ranging from over 65 percent of the agreements for the Truman administration to only 46 percent for the Nixon administration. Conversely, an overall rise in ties took place with authoritarian states, from about 32 percent for the Truman and Johnson administrations to about 46 percent for the Nixon years.

International Agreements from the Cold War to Détente

Table 9
Regime Targets of U.S. Foreign Agreements by Administration, 1946–1972

	Administration				
Regime Type	Truman	Eisenhower	Kennedy	Johnson	Nixon
Democratic					
% of agreements	65.4[a]	61.5	55.4	53.2	45.8
% of states	48.0[b]	43.0	50.4	46.1	41.8
Difference	+17.4[c]	+18.5	+ 5.0	+ 7.1	+ 4.0
Authoritarian					
% of agreements	32.2	35.0	40.8	39.9	46.0
% of states	38.7	43.0	35.9	41.4	44.8
Difference	− 6.5	− 8.0	+ 4.9	− 1.5	+ 1.2
Totalitarian					
% of agreements	2.4	3.5	3.8	6.9	8.2
% of states	13.3	14.0	13.7	12.5	13.4
Difference	−10.9	−10.5	− 9.9	− 5.6	− 5.2
(N)	(1,120)	(1,728)	(711)	(977)	(793)

[a] Entries are percentages based on Column Ns shown at the bottom. Multilateral agreements and agreements with dependent territories are not included here.
[b] The "% of states" refers to the relative distribution of democratic, authoritarian, and totalitarian regimes during each administration. For a discussion of how this figure was calculated, see note 4.
[c] A plus sign indicates that more agreements were signed with the regime type than might be expected, given the distribution of the three regime types in the international system; a negative sign indicates the converse.

In terms of percentage, though certainly not in terms of total numbers, the ties with Marxist states registered the most dramatic change—more than tripling from about 2 percent of the total for the first postwar administration to over 8 percent for the Johnson and Nixon presidencies. The center of gravity in U.S. foreign policy thus shifted perceptibly toward autocracies and away from democracies; nonetheless, our bonds with other democratic states continued to remain preeminent.

This perspective, however, fails to account for fluctuations in the number of new regimes that came into being during the postwar years. It obviously matters precisely how many democratic, authoritarian, and totalitarian states an administration had

In Search of Friends: America's Agreement Partners

available from which to choose friends in any given year. To provide a more complete picture of the distribution of United States foreign commitments abroad, the percentage of the three regime-types available for each administration was calculated (see table 9).

By using this information, one can adjust for the relative change in the size and political characteristics of the international system when assessing the tendency for an administration to make agreements with each regime type. This adjustment allows the analyst to determine whether the increased frequency of agreements with autocracies under Presidents Johnson and Nixon, for example, was merely a function of the proliferation in numbers of such regimes during the postcolonial period.

Using this control, it was found that all five administrations had a greater percentage of agreements with democracies than might have been expected. The Truman and Eisenhower administrations were especially high, with 17 percent and 19 percent greater than the percentage of democratic states in the international system. By contrast, the Nixon and Kennedy administrations were the lowest, with only 4 and 5 percent more agreements than might be anticipated. The Johnson administration was in between, with roughly 7 percent more agreements than might be expected.

Ties with authoritarian states fluctuated from 8 and 7 percent below what would be expected for the Eisenhower and Truman administrations to about 5 percent above for the Kennedy administration. The other administrations were generally close to what might be anticipated, with Nixon above and Johnson slightly below. On average, though, authoritarian states had somewhat fewer agreements with the United States than what would be expected, given their relative numbers within the international system.

In sum, in terms of total percentages (the first level of anal-

International Agreements from the Cold War to Détente

ysis), democracies have been our principal partners for international commitments; in terms of adjusted percentages (the second level of analysis), the United States has still always embraced other democracies more often than what might be anticipated by simply extrapolating from their relative proportion within the international system. In total percentages, international agreements with authoritarian states increased during the Nixon administration but, in all administrations, continued to rank second behind democracies. Taking into account the relative distribution of regime types during each administration, the authoritarian states tended to be the objects of a greater percentage of agreements than their numbers alone would predict since about 1960.

What stood out most starkly in the analysis, though, was the few ties between the United States and totalitarian states. These commitments constituted a small percentage of our total pacts abroad over the years, and they were below what one might predict based on the number of these states in the world. The United States did sign sixty-four international agreements with the Soviet Union, however. While that number is large in comparison to other totalitarian states (Yugoslavia excepted), the Soviet Union nonetheless ranks below the top 20 percent of America's agreement partners. In its selection of partners, the United States has shown a decided preference for its neighbors in the western hemisphere and for nations on the perimeter of the communist Eurasian land mass (see figure 3).

Regimes and Policy Content

Next the agreement targets were examined from the perspective of the five different policy areas captured by the data. As table 10 indicates, the democratic states outdistanced authoritarian and totalitarian regimes as targets within all the content areas. For democracies, the most popular policy commitments were military, transportation-communication, and

Figure 3
America's Major Agreement Partners: Twenty-Seven Countries Most Frequently Targeted for Bilateral Pacts (the Top Twenty Percent), 1946–73.

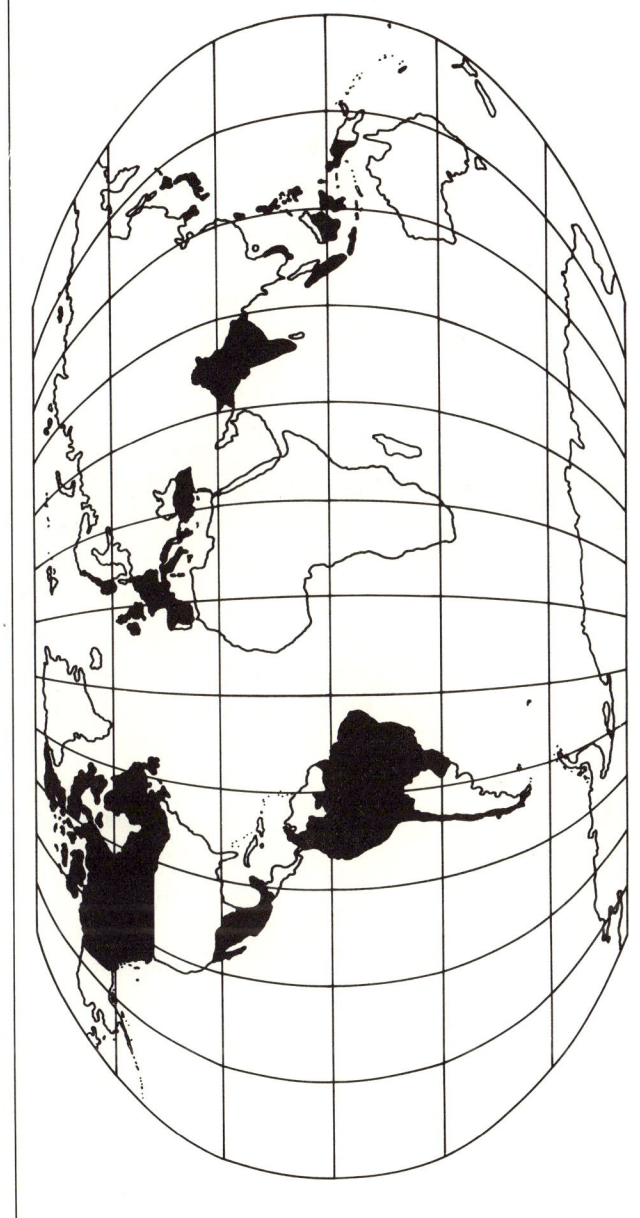

International Agreements from the Cold War to Détente

diplomatic. Democratic states were targets for an average of 65 percent or more of such commitments; within the remaining two policy areas, the democratic states continued to predominate, with over 50 percent of the agreements. In this sense, then, democracies constituted a majority percentage of the targets in the 1946 to 1973 period, regardless of the policy content of the commitments.

These policy commitments were then examined across each of the regime types. Economic pacts were the most popular form of association between the United States and other states, regardless of regime type. Over 1,000 economic commitments were made with democracies, over 860 with authoritarian states, and over 100 with totalitarian states. In each instance, such totals exceeded agreements in the other policy areas by a wide margin, especially for the authoritarian and totalitarian states. With each of the other policy areas, the democracies always had the greatest number of agreements, but the authoritarian states had the same order of priority as the democracies: cultural-technical, military, transportation-communication, and diplomatic. By contrast, the ties between America and totalitarian states have tended to emphasize cultural-technical, diplomatic, and transportation-communication links. As might be expected, military ties between the United States and totalitarian regimes were rare.

In sum, then, while democracies dominate America's ties across the policy areas, the patterns of linkage between the United States, on the one hand, and democratic and authoritarian states, on the other, parallel one another and differ only in magnitude. By contrast, American links with totalitarian states differ both in volume and in the pattern of commitments—at least beyond the economic agreements, which held highest priority for every regime.

These patterns tended to hold when each administration was examined separately. Democracies were the most prominent

In Search of Friends: America's Agreement Partners

Table 10
Regime Targets of U.S. Bilateral Agreements by Five Policy Areas, 1946–1972

Regime Type	Policy				
	Military	Economic	Transportation-Communication	Cultural-Technical	Diplomatic
Democratic states	64.7%[a]	50.9%	67.2%	55.8%	66.3%
Authoritarian states	33.3	43.2	27.8	41.0	22.4
Totalitarian states	2.0	5.9	4.9	3.2	11.2
(N)	(1,076)	(1,994)	(528)	(1,394)	(312)

[a] Entries are percentages based on column Ns shown at bottom. Twenty-five agreements, representing 0.5% of the total, were classified as "Other" for content and are not shown in the table.

partners across all policy areas. The exceptions were for economic and diplomatic policies. For the former, the percentage of agreements with democracies fell below 50 percent for the Kennedy, Johnson, and Nixon administrations. As a consequence, the authoritarian states were the dominant economic partners for these administrations. Moreover, for the Nixon years, about 56 percent of the economic pacts were with authoritarian states and only 38 percent were with democracies. Similarly, in the Nixon administration, the percentage of diplomatic pacts for democracies fell below 50 percent to about 42 percent. This percentage, though, was still the highest among the three regime types. In short, while democracies generally continued to be primary targets for most policy areas during each of the five postwar presidencies, the highest percentage of economic ties were with authoritarian states for the three most recent (Kennedy through Nixon). When it came to international economic policy, since 1960 the United States apparently became less philosophically fastidious in its selection of partners.

International Agreements from the Cold War to Détente

Regime Types, the President, and the Congress

Who was primarily responsible for cementing these pacts with democratic, authoritarian, and totalitarian regimes? To what extent did the president and the Congress share in the targeting? Most American bilateral commitments, it turns out, took the form of statutory agreements, rather than treaties or executive agreements. Overall, 86 percent or more of American bilateral agreements for each presidency took this form. So, both the Congress and the executive have been involved in the agreement-making process. Despite the preponderance of the statutory form, some important patterns emerge and reflect the differential effect of regime type upon the bonding form selected for commitment-making.

As already emphasized, agreements with democratic states were predominant for each form of international commitment. A closer examination of the agreements with democracies reveals that, across administrations, the treaty percentages are systematically higher than statutory or executive agreement percentages (table 11). This result suggests that the treaty tends to be a more popular form of commitment with democratic states.

Clear trends in agreement form also existed for the making of commitments with the other two regime types. Across all administrations, the most popular means of "tying the knot" with authoritarian states was the statutory agreement. Moreover, each of the five administrations used this form most often in reaching agreements with authoritarian states, even though this procedure involves both houses of Congress. Perhaps the sometimes controversial nature of authoritarian regimes discouraged attempts toward agreement-making by full-blown treaty process, and the volume of these pacts may have been considered too great to claim executive-agreement authority for fear of provoking congressional ire.

The greatest percentage of ties with totalitarian states took

Table 11
Regime Targets of U.S. Foreign Agreements by Form for Five Administrations, 1946–1972

	Administration and Form																		
	Truman			Eisenhower			Kennedy			Johnson			Nixon			Total		
Regime Type	T[a]	EA	SA	T	EA	SA	T	EA	SA	T	EA	SA	T	EA	SA	T	EA	SA
Democratic states	82.2[b]	67.9	64.3	81.6	79.3	59.9	85.7	77.8	53.9	87.5	72.0	50.9	68.4	54.3	44.2	81.1	69.6	56.0
Authoritarian states	17.8	28.6	33.3	18.4	14.9	36.6	14.3	14.8	42.4	6.3	13.4	43.0	26.3	20.0	49.7	17.5	19.6	39.8
Totalitarian states	0.0	3.6	2.4	0.0	5.7	3.5	0.0	7.4	3.7	6.3	14.6	6.1	5.3	25.7	6.1	1.4	10.8	4.2
(N)	(45)	(112)	(963)	(49)	(87)	(1,592)	(14)	(27)	(670)	(16)	(82)	(876)	(19)	(70)	(692)	(143)	(378)	(4,793)

[a] T = treaty, EA = Executive Agreement, SA = Statutory Agreement.
[b] Entries are percentages based on column Ns shown at bottom.

the form of executive agreements. This form of bonding does not require congressional participation and thus makes it easier to establish commitments overseas without the difficulty of confronting the legislative branch. The executive branch may see this approach as a boon in dealing with Marxist regimes, since they are few in number and are often viewed by some members of Congress as especially incompatible with American values.

In sum, then, statutory agreements dominated the entire process of American agreement-making. Beyond this proposition, one notes that the treaty was more likely to be the favored instrument for dealing with democracies, the statutory agreement for authoritarian regimes, and the executive agreement for totalitarian regimes.

Regimes and International Agreements: A Summary

The central point about American regime targets is this: throughout the period from 1946 to 1973, our country has exhibited a strong partiality toward democracies around the world—despite the existence of an international system in which democracies have usually represented a minority of states. Looking at United States agreements across the board (that is, in every policy area), each administration from Truman through Nixon established more ties with democracies than with either authoritarian or totalitarian regimes. Moreover, with the exception of the Nixon administration, these ties with democracies always outnumbered the total for the two autocracies combined. (Forty-six percent of the Nixon international agreements were with democracies, while 54 percent were with dictatorships; see table 9.) The democratic birds have normally flocked together, a result presumably of greater ideological affinity and closer compatibility in stages of economic growth.

In spite of this affinity for nations that share our fundamental belief in free elections and a competitive industrial society, the

In Search of Friends: America's Agreement Partners

United States has entered into a large number of wide-ranging commitments with authoritarian regimes (our second most popular global partners). If we have preferred democracies (especially for military pacts), we have certainly been less than shy about seeking bonds with right-wing dictators when they might serve our purposes. In the area of economic policy, for instance, the United States showed a strong preference for authoritarian regimes even over democracies during the Kennedy, Johnson, and Nixon administrations. This is a reflection partially, no doubt, of continuing American interest in raw materials, low-cost labor, and burgeoning new markets in the populous developing world. The economic bond, in short, has been the essential cohesion between us and authoritarian states in the conduct of American foreign policy. On matters of military security, then, our instincts have been to place trust chiefly in the democracies; on matters of the pocketbook, though, we have been prepared to seek our fortunes almost wherever they may be found.

One must say "almost" since in every policy area—including trade—the United States has largely viewed the totalitarian regimes as anathemas. Presuambly the anti-Marxist ideological baggage toted by virtually every policy-maker (assuredly the elected ones), and most Americans, has discouraged overtures toward this part of the globe. In recent years, the United States has resorted to the extreme measure of boycotts and embargoes much more frequently against totalitarian states than authoritarian states (though, to be sure, we have also engaged in an opening of relations with the People's Republic of China and ongoing trade with Angola).

Finally, the president and Congress have largely shared responsibility in shaping American commitments to the three different regime types. The use of the statutory form has been prominent across authoritarian, totalitarian, and democratic regimes. Despite such executive-legislative participation in the great number of pacts, some notable differences exist in the use of different forms within each regime type. The treaty was the form used most often with democracies, the statutory agreement with authoritarian regimes, and the executive agreement with totalitarian regimes. In this sense, more executive discretion was allowed for the agreements with autocratic states, especially totalitarian ones.

Regions and Foreign Policy Commitments

A second way in which the agreement partners of the United States were assessed was to examine the commitments by region. First all bilateral pacts were categorized into one of six different geographical regions: Western Europe (including Canada, Sweden, Finland, Austria, and the rest of the Atlantic Alliance); Eastern Europe (the USSR and its alliance partners); the Middle East (the Arab states, Israel, and Northern Africa); Latin America; Africa; and Asia. (Appendix B shows a country-by-country breakdown for each region.)

According to the analysis, three regions have dominated the agreement-making of the United States in the postwar period: Western Europe, with 29 percent of the pacts; Latin America, with 26 percent; and Asia, with 23 percent. The other regions of the world were rarely recipients of many American commitments. When regional agreements were examined by administration, moreover, the dominance of these three regions remained for each presidency though not always in the same order (see table 12). The percentage of agreements with Western Europe declined from a high of 38 percent of all pacts under President Truman to only 19 percent during President Nixon's first four years in office. A similar decline is evident for Latin America across the presidents, with 35 percent for President Truman but only 17 and 23 percents for Presidents Johnson and Nixon. The region that increased in the volume of agreements over time was Asia. To a considerable extent, this increase is attributable

In Search of Friends: America's Agreement Partners

Table 12
Region Targets of U.S. Foreign Agreements by Administration, 1946–1972

	Administration				
Region	Truman	Eisenhower	Kennedy	Johnson	Nixon
Latin America[a]	35.0%[b]	27.7%	24.9%	17.1%	22.8%
Western Europe	38.0	32.5	25.2	25.2	19.2
Middle East	8.1	12.2	12.9	12.4	11.0
Africa	2.8	2.7	9.8	11.7	5.9
Eastern Europe	2.3	3.5	3.4	5.7	8.2
Asia	13.8	21.5	23.8	27.9	32.9
(N)	(1,120)	(1,728)	(711)	(977)	(793)

[a] See the text and the appendix for countries included in each region.
[b] Entries are percentages based on columns Ns shown at bottom. All percentages do not add to 100 due to rounding error.

to the increasing ties with Southeast Asian states during the period of the Vietnam War.

The failure of the other regions to gain much in the percentage of American ties in the postwar years is striking in light of the "globalism" that seemed to pervade America's foreign policy pronouncements. Instead, what appeared to happen was a leveling-out of agreement partners located in Western Europe, Latin America, and Asia, but without much increase in ties with the Middle East, Africa, and Eastern Europe. Overall, then, one concludes that there has been a remarkable stability in the regional partnerships selected by the United States in its foreign policy commitments from 1946 to 1973.

Region, Policy, and Form of American Agreements

When the policy content of American agreements was analyzed by region, no substantial departures from the earlier analysis were discovered. For each policy area, as shown in table 13, Western Europe, Latin America, and Asia were America's most popular regional partners. We have turned, for ex-

International Agreements from the Cold War to Détente

Table 13
Regional Priorities of U.S. Foreign Agreements by Content Area, 1946–1972

Total	Military	Economic	Transportation-Communication	Cultural-Technical	Diplomatic
Western Europe (29.4%)[a]	Western Europe (41.6%)	Asia (30.3%)	Western Europe (38.6%)	Latin America (41.0%)	Western Europe (38.5%)
Latin America (26.2)	Latin America (22.8)	Western Europe (23.5)	Latin America (28.0)	Western Europe (22.2)	Asia (22.1)
Asia (23.0)	Asia (22.4)	Latin America (18.6)	Asia (18.6)	Asia (15.1)	Latin America (18.9)
Middle East (11.3)	Middle East (7.9)	Middle East (15.4)	Middle East (6.3)	Middle East (11.7)	Eastern Europe (10.9)
Africa (5.8)	Africa (3.3)	Africa (6.5)	Eastern Europe (4.7)	Africa (7.5)	Africa (5.4)
Eastern Europe (4.4)	Eastern Europe (2.0)	Eastern Europe (5.1)	Africa (3.8)	Eastern Europe (2.5)	Middle East (4.2)
(5,329)	(1,076)	(1,994)	(528)	(1,394)	(312)

[a] Entries are percentages based on column Ns. Twenty-five agreements (0.5% of the total) were classified as "Other" for content and are not shown in the five content columns. Percentages do not always add to 100 due to rounding error.

See the text and the appendix for countries included in each region.

ample, to Western Europe most often for pacts on military security, transportation and communication, and diplomatic issues; to Asia for trade and economic ties; and to Latin America for cultural-technical agreements. We have tended to ignore, relatively speaking, the Middle East and—particularly—Africa. And, as one would expect, the region of least contact has been Soviet-dominated Eastern Europe.

In Search of Friends: America's Agreement Partners

The preponderance of the three main regions of American commitments (Western Europe, Latin America, and Asia) is more fully illustrated by calculating the combined percentage of these areas for each policy category. These three regions constituted over 85 percent of the agreements in the military and transportation-communication policy areas, and more than 78 percent of the pacts in the cultural-technical and diplomatic areas. The lowest percentage for these three regions was in the economic area, in which they still accounted for fully 72 percent of the pacts. American economic ties are slightly—but only slightly— more widely distributed in the world than are the other kinds of policy agreements.

Analyzing policy content by regional priorities across the five administrations, a small decline was detected in the dominance of Western Europe, Latin America, and Asia. For all policies, the percentage of agreements within these regions has undergone a decline from President Truman to President Nixon. While President Truman averaged about 88 percent of his agreements with these areas of the world, by the end of 1972 President Nixon was averaging 72 percent of his agreements with these regions. The diplomatic policy areas had the lowest ties with these three regions (63 percent of the pacts), while by the seventies military policy produced the highest percentage of pacts. In this sense, some broadening of America's regional agreement partners has taken place over the twenty-seven years of our study, but what remains most striking—even in this context of change— is the highly consistent pattern of commitment-making on the part of the United States.

Finally, the form of agreement-making within each region was studied. As expected, the statutory agreement dominated the initiation of commitments to all regions. For no region did the use of the statutory agreement fall below 81 percent (see table 14); for three regions (Latin America, the Middle East, and Africa), roughly 94 percent or more of the international agreements took the statutory form. By contrast, the treaty form is

International Agreements from the Cold War to Détente

Table 14
The Use of Three Forms of Agreement-Making Within Six Global Regions

Form	Latin America	Western Europe	Middle East	Africa	Eastern Europe	Asia
Treaty	1.5%[a]	5.0%	1.0%	1.6%	.9%	2.5%
Executive agreement	4.2	9.3	2.5	4.9	18.1	8.5
Statutory agreement	94.3	85.7	96.5	93.5	81.1	89.0
(N)	(1,392)	(1,563)	(600)	(307)	(227)	(1,225)

[a] Entries are percentages based on column Ns. Twenty-five agreements (0.5% of the total) were excluded from the analysis because Department of State classification could not be obtained. Multilateral agreements and agreements with dependent territories are not included here.

rarely used. In fact, only one region (Western Europe) has more than 3 percent of its commitments in the treaty form. With such results, one again must emphasize that, in terms of sheer quantity, the Congress and the president have shared agreement-making toward the various regions of the world—though by way of the arguably less demanding legislative review inherent in the statutory agreement (as contrasted to the treaty process, with its requirement of a two-thirds majority).

Nonetheless, a significant number—if not a large percentage—of international commitments are handled by executive agreement. The percentage of such pacts ranged from only about 3 percent for commitments in the Middle East to 18 percent for commitments in Eastern Europe. A closer inspection of these executive agreements by content reveals, moreover, that military and diplomatic policies had the highest percentage of such pacts for each of the six global regions—with the highest percentages for Eastern Europe, Asia, and Africa. Analysis by administration produced comparable findings. Thus, as discovered in chapter 1, military and diplomatic policies seem particularly susceptible to executive discretion. In this regard, a further scrutiny of these pacts (in the next chapter) seems especially warranted.

In Search of Friends: America's Agreement Partners

In sum, the regional findings are generally consistent with the regime findings with respect to executive-legislative involvement in the commitment of the United States abroad. American agreements with Eastern Europe, a region comprised of totalitarian states, have been reached chiefly through the instrument of the executive agreement; those with Asia, the Middle East, and Africa, regions chiefly authoritarian, through the statutory agreement; and, those with Western Europe, a region chiefly democratic, through the treaty.

Principal Nations and Foreign Policy Commitments

In this portion of the study, the focus turns toward the key nations that have served as foreign policy partners for the United States in the postwar years. The objective here is to identify specifically the major American alliance partners and to examine the form and content of agreements reached with these nations. In effect, the research tries to ascertain whether the Congress and the president departed from the norm in the agreement process when dealing with the most important nations to American foreign policy.

Although 89 percent of all American agreements in the postwar period have been bilateral commitments, relatively few nations have served as agreement targets for the United States. Fourteen nations have been the recipients of 1,931 American foreign policy commitments, a number equivalent to 36 percent of all bilateral agreements and 32 percent of all American commitments for the years of this analysis.[5] (These fourteen nations are presented in table 15.)

In the postwar period, the United Kingdom, Canada, and Japan have been the primary agreement partners of the United States. In addition, though, four other member of NATO have been among the principal partners for the United States. So, as one might expect from the aggregate regime and region anal-

Table 15
Most Favored Targets for U.S. Agreements, 1946–1972

Nation	Number of Agreements	Rank
United Kingdom	205	1
Canada	199	2
Japan	168	3
Philippines	148	4
Mexico	144	5.5
Brazil	144	5.5
Republic of China	134	7
South Korea	124	8
France	120	9
West Germany	116	10
Italy	113	11
Pakistan	112	12
Turkey	103	13
Peru	101	14

yses, the most important partners have been chiefly Western European democracies.

At the same time, two other key regions are represented. Latin America (with Mexico, Peru, and Brazil) and Asia (with the Philippines, Japan, the Republic of China, the Republic of Korea, and Pakistan) also appear among the leading agreement partners. The presence of these states on the "List of Fourteen" reflects the degree to which authoritarian regimes (Japan excluded) have been a crucial part of America's postwar efforts toward wooing allies abroad.

Form, Content, and Principal Partners

To assess whether agreements with key partners of the United States differed in policy content and form from the entire survey, these two dimensions were examined for only the fourteen principal countries. (The results are shown in table 16.)

The policy content of the agreements for these states focused mainly on economic commitments (33 percent), with military

In Search of Friends: America's Agreement Partners

Table 16
Form and Content of U.S. Agreements with Most Favored Target Nations, 1946–1972

	Content				
Form	Military	Economic	Transportation-Communications	Cultural-Technical	Diplomatic
Executive agreements	13.7%[a]	7.0%	6.7%	5.8%	26.4%
Statutory agreements	84.1	87.5	91.4	92.5	62.0
Treaties	2.2	5.5	1.9	1.7	11.6
(N)	(496)	(598)	(210)	(481)	(129)

[a] Entries are percentages based on the column Ns. Thirteen agreements (0.7% of the total) were classified as "Other" for those fourteen nations and are not included in the table.

pacts ranked second (27 percent) and cultural-technical ties third (27 percent). Transportation-communication and diplomatic agreements were much lower in volume, at 7 percent and 6 percent, respectively. The emphasis upon economic pacts is consistent with the overall analysis, albeit at a considerably lower percentage. The percentage of military pacts, however, was 8 percent higher than for the total agreements examined in chapter 1. In this sense, the importance of military ties with America's key partners is clear.

At the same time, the cultural-technical ties were below what had been the overall pattern with the entire data set (27 percent compared to an earlier 34 percent). Similarly, the lower percentage of transportation-communication pacts illustrates the difference in content of agreements with key political allies of the United States compared to the world as a whole. The percentage of diplomatic pacts in the entire data set and in the fourteen nations subset is, however, about the same. In sum, the policy content of America's commitments to its key partners took a decidedly more military thrust than witnessed for all agreement partners in the postwar period.

International Agreements from the Cold War to Détente

The use of the three agreement forms also differed with the List of Fourteen, compared with the overall patterns presented earlier. While statutory agreements were used a consistent 86 percent of the time on the average (compared to 87 percent for the entire data set), treaties were used at a lower rate with these special nations than with the total (4 percent compared to 6 percent). Similarly, and perhaps most significantly, the executive agreement form was used 10 percent of the time for the Fourteen (3 percent higher than the overall average). Furthermore, similar to what has been seen throughout this survey, the military and diplomatic agreements with the Fourteen had a higher percentage of executive agreements than any other policy area.

A Recapitulation

Several conclusions emerge from this survey of America's agreement partners during the 1946–1972 period. First, the United States has tended to enter into agreements chiefly with democratic nations. Only in the most recent administrations of the survey have authoritarian states begun to rival, in number, democracies as agreement partners for this country. For each of the five different policy areas, this general pattern holds true.

This portrait of American alignments abroad is rather different from that portrayed in recent nonempirical analyses. The widely read observations of UN Ambassador Jeane J. Kirkpatrick, for example, fail to acknowledge adequately our strong and pervasive ties to democratic states—the very hallmark of America's postwar policy.[6] Any assessment of agreement-making by the United States abroad must recognize the way in which our behavior has been guided chiefly by an attraction for kindred political and economic values. While criticizing the administration of President Jimmy Carter (1976–1980) for overtures toward Marxist regimes (especially the Sandinistas of Nicaragua),

In Search of Friends: America's Agreement Partners

Kirkpatrick leaves the false impression that postwar American foreign policy has flirted too often and ruinously with leftist regimes. In fact, the evidence shows that links between the United States and totalitarian states have been few and weak, at least from 1946 to 1973 and perhaps beyond.

Closer to the mark is the more fundamental thesis in Kirkpatrick's commentary on American ties with autocrats: this country has consistently preferred ties (of all varieties) with dictators of the right. Whether this approach is ethically proper or even beneficial to us as a nation is a separate matter; the fact remains that this is the choice made during the quarter century following World War II. The "Tito gambit," in which the United States attempted (perhaps with some success) to dampen Yugoslavia's adherence to Moscow-Marxist doctrine by holding out alluring economic inducements in the West, has been—so this data suggest—a policy used in the most limited way. The strategy of détente devised by Henry Kissinger, President Nixon's National Security Advisor and, later, his Secretary of State, may have been intended, in theory, to enact a web of interlocking agreements with totalitarian states as a way of reducing their revolutionary fervor; in reality, however, this research has found no evidence to indicate the growth of such agreements. What we have been more inclined to do, evidently, is to keep the Marxists at arm's length, even if this meant shoving them into the arms of the Soviets.[7]

One can only speculate about the possible effects on world politics of an effort by the United States to go beyond the rhetoric of détente toward more tangible increases in international agreements with totalitarian regimes. One suspects the experiment would be safe, and even helpful; our circle of friendships could enlarge. The empirical findings here demonstrate a disequilibrium in American foreign policy commitments. One's normative hunch is that efforts toward greater equilibrium in American commitments—reaching out toward those we have cast aside—could only benefit the United States. Enhanced trade with the totalitarian states is only the most obvious example.

A second conclusion is related to the regional findings: the overwhelming majority of American ties have been located in three regions: Western Europe, Latin America, and Asia. When policy areas and administration were examined, these regional priorities remained.

Third, the empirical analysis of America's principal agreement partners confirms what many might have intuitively suspected. The United Kingdom, Canada, and Japan ranked highest in the total number of pacts with the United States. Still, the top fourteen nations favored by America for international commitments contained a broad distribution of nations from Western Europe, Latin America, and Asia. Our key partners abroad have not been confined to the Western Alliance, as conventional wisdom would often have it.

Finally, and most crucial for the overall examination of Congress and the presidency in foreign policy, important trends were discovered in the use of the three major instruments of agreement-making. The statutory agreement dominated the process, whether analyzed by regime, region, or favored nations; the treaty was little used. Of greatest significance, the executive agreement was used at a much greater rate than the other forms for military and diplomatic policy-making.

In further pursuit of this last finding, the analysis turns now to inspect in greater detail the qualitative nature of those agreements made in the postwar period by recourse to assumed executive authority. In particular, the research concentrates on military commitments, since they are likely to be the most far-reaching for American policy abroad.

Notes

1. On the distinction between authoritarian and totalitarian regimes, see Roy Macridis, *Contemporary Political Ideologies: Movements and Regimes*

In Search of Friends: America's Agreement Partners

(Cambridge, Massachusetts: Winthrop Publishers, 1980), especially pp. 223–225. Also see the recent press commentaries: Michael Levin, "How to Tell Bad From Worse," *Newsweek*, July 20, 1981, p. 7; and Hans Koning, "Free to Go to the Devil," *The New York Times*, July 6, 1981, p. 19. (For the totalitarian regime category, also coded into this group were those states that were closely allied with the Soviet Union, even though the Communist party requirement might not be fully met.) Finally, see Jeane J. Kirkpatrick, "Dictatorships and Double Standards," *Commentary* 68 (November 1979), pp. 34–45.

2. These volumes were published by McGraw-Hill (New York, 1976) and the Government Printing Office (Washington, D.C., 1978), respectively.

3. The 645 multilateral agreements and 42 agreements with dependent territories are excluded from this part of the analysis. The percentages are based upon the bilateral agreement totals only.

4. To identify the relative percentage of nations within each regime category, first the number of nations in the international system for the *median* year of each administration were identified: 1949 for the Truman administration; 1957 for the Eisenhower administration; 1962 for the Kennedy administration; 1966 for the Johnson administration; and, 1970 for the Nixon administration. The following sources were used to obtain the number of independent nations in these *median* years: A. Leroy Bennett, *International Organizations: Principles and Issues* (Englewood Cliffs, N.J.: Prentice-Hall, 1980), appendix, pp. 509–514; Bruce Russett and Harvey Starr, *World Politics: The Menu for Choice* (San Francisco: W. H. Freeman, 1981), appendix B, pp. 575–583; and David J. Finlay and Thomas Hovet, Jr., *7304: International Relations on the Planet Earth* (New York: Harper and Row, 1975), pp. 24–25. The last source was particularly useful, since it contained a chronological listing of newly independent nations. As a consequence, the number of member nations for each administration from Truman to Nixon could be calculated incrementally. For each *median* year ranking, the nations were coded into the three regimes based upon the earlier regime classification. From that calculation, the percentage of nations that were democratic, authoritarian, and totalitarian in the world could be derived for each administration.

5. Fourteen nations were chosen for further analysis, since they represented those nations with more than 100 agreements with the United States in the 1946–1973 period.

6. Kirkpatrick, op. cit., p. 44.

7. See J. William Fulbright, "Reflections: U.S. Foreign Policy Since 1945," *The New Yorker* 47 (January 8, 1972), pp. 41–62.

3.

The Hidden Side of Agreement-Making

> . . . in action after action, responsibility for decision is as fluid and restless as quicksilver, and there seems to be neither a person nor an organization on whom it can be fixed. At times the point of decision seems to have escaped into the labyrinth of governmental machinery, beyond layers and layers of bureaucracy.
>
> —ROGER HILSMAN, *To Move a Nation*

Foreign Policy by Sleight of Hand

The executive agreement can be an elusive instrument of foreign policy-making, used to engage the United States in commitments abroad with little (if any) public debate. In a 1972 report, members of the Senate Foreign Relations Committee noted: "As the committee has discovered, there have been numerous agreements contracted with foreign governments in recent years, particularly agreements of a military nature, which remain wholly unknown to Congress and to the people. . . ."[1] This chapter focuses more sharply on the use of executive

The Hidden Side of Agreement-Making

agreements for the binding of the United States to other nations, especially in the area of military, diplomatic, and intelligence obligations. These often secret compacts represent a serious challenge to the democratic control of foreign policy and, indeed, to the fundamental principles of a free society.

Military Agreements: An Overview

In the crucible of war, the Constitution takes on malleable properties. President Abraham Lincoln's expansive interpretation of the commander-in-chief clause during the Civil War is a well-known case in point. More recently, World War II and the protracted Cold War profoundly altered the shape of foreign policy: as the nation embraced strong leadership to thwart external threats, power shifted dramatically to the presidency.

This aggrandizement is reflected in the startling number of overseas military commitments since the end of World War II that have been grounded in claims of inherent executive authority. The executive branch has, among other things, placed military personnel in Guatemala, Mainland China, Ethiopia, and Iran; pledged military support to Turkey, Iran, Pakistan, and, on the eve of war, South Korea; and contracted for military bases in Spain, the Azores, the Philippines, Diego Garcia, and Bahrain. Beneath this tip of the iceberg lies an expanse of executive discretion in peacetime foreign policy that reaches alarming proportions.

As shown at the beginning of this book, only 7 percent of all formal commitments entered into by the United States abroad from 1946 to 1973 were based on executive agreements. Although this form represents a small percentage of the total, executive agreements have sometimes been more significant than treaties. The central question of interest here is: How often has the Congress been excluded from decisions about crucial commitments abroad?

International Agreements from the Cold War to Détente

"There is no known qualitative analysis of the relative importance of the treaties and executive agreements now in force," writes John B. Rehm.[2] This portion of the study attempts partially to address this shortcoming through a qualitative review of American military commitments overseas during the Cold War, for these obligations have proved to be especially controversial and costly (the placement of troops and weapons abroad—so-called "forward deployment"—adds up to the most expensive portion of the American military budget). The analysis concentrates solely on the use of treaties and executive agreements since, though less frequently used, they have become far more contentious than statutory agreements.

Nineteen percent of the international agreements during the 1946–1973 period involved military matters. An inspection of the content of these agreements reveals two general types: substantive and administrative. Substantive military agreements deal with the creation of military alliances, the signing of peace treaties, the establishment of military bases, the disposal of military equipment, and the like. Administrative agreements deal with secondary details, such as the establishment of a military headquarters based on an alliance, personnel staffing, and the like. For the purposes of this study, the substantive agreements are considered "significant," because they commit this country to specific policy positions; the administrative agreements are "insignificant," because they deal with housekeeping matters. Among the 1,146 military commitments concluded between January 1, 1946, and December 31, 1972, 41 (or about 4 percent) were in the form of treaties, 963 (or 84 percent) were statutory agreements, and 142 (or about 12 percent) were executive agreements. The subject matter of the 183 treaties and executive agreements were examined to assess their relative significance.

The conventional wisdom—at least on Capitol Hill—suggests that the advice and consent of the Senate has been requested

The Hidden Side of Agreement-Making

by the executive branch largely for policies with little substantive meaning. Some justification exists for this view. In 1978, Senator Dick Clark (D, Iowa) complained on the Senate floor that "the treaty form has been used for a shrimp agreement with Brazil, an agreement on the conservation on [sic] polar bears, and an agreement regarding the uninhabited coral reefs in the Caribbean."[3] Other treaties have dealt with such momentous topics as the recovery of lost archaeological objects in Mexico,[4] an increase in membership of the International Atomic Energy Board from 25 to 34 or 35,[5] and the international classification of industrial designs.[6]

The findings here (presented in table 17) indicate, however, that treaties in the post–World War II period have been used mainly for important military commitments, not for trivial matters. Of the 41 military treaties signed in the administrations from Presidents Truman through Nixon, 32 (or 78 percent) dealt with major defense obligations. Among them were various se-

Table 17
The Dominance of Executive Agreements over Treaties in the Making of Significant Military Commitments Abroad, 1946–1972[a]

Administration	Significant Military Treaties (T)	Significant Military Executive Agreements (EA)	Executive Agreement Index $EA/(T+EA)$[b]
Truman	16	28	.64
Eisenhower	6	30	.83
Kennedy	1	4	.80
Johnson	5	24	.83
Nixon	4	13	.76
Total	32	99	

[a]This table summarizes the use of military treaties and executive agreements only; statutory agreements, which are more numerous but less controversial, are not analyzed here.

[b]The numbers in this column represent for each administration the proportion of significant military executive agreements, compared to the total number of significant military treaties and executive agreements. This Executive Agreement Index ranges from 0 to 1; the higher the index, the greater the reliance on executive agreements for major military commitments.

International Agreements from the Cold War to Détente

curity arrangements with Japan, the Republic of Korea, and the nations of Western Europe; major arms control accords, including the nuclear test ban treaty of 1963; and postwar peace treaties with former belligerents (for example, the treaty of peace with Italy). Nine of the treaties (22 percent) excluded from the "significant" category dealt with administrative details of major defense pacts, most notably the North Atlantic Treaty Organization. In short, the evidence—at any rate for defense commitments abroad—fails to support the conventional wisdom. Treaties really have not been banished from their traditional role.

Senators Fulbright, Case, and others may have been close to the mark, however, with their complaints about the use of executive agreements for negotiating important military commitments (see chapter 1). Although some 43 of the 142 military executive agreements dealing with military matters in this postwar period were indeed routine and minor (dealing with such issues as the establishment of a practice bombing range in West Germany and reciprocal air rights with Canada for rescue operations), a striking number involved major commitments abroad. The following obligations were entered into partly or completely on the basis of an assertion of executive authority:

- use of the Azores airbases by the United States (1947)
- placement of United States troops in Guatemala (1947)
- establishment of United States bases in the Philippines (1947)
- placement of United States troops in Mainland China (1948)
- military security in the Republic of Korea (1949)
- United States military mission in Honduras (1950)
- broad United States military prerogatives in Ethiopia (1953)
- United States military mission to El Salvador (1957)
- United States military mission to Liberia (1958)

The Hidden Side of Agreement-Making

- United States base rights in Lebanon (1958)
- security pledges to Turkey, Iran, and Pakistan (1959)
- military use of the British island Diego Garcia (1966)
- military use of Bahrain (1971)
- agreement terminating military and economic pact with Libya (1972)

Seventy percent (99 of 142) of the military agreements signed during this period were judged to represent significant commitments abroad that seemed to merit closer scrutiny by the legislative branch. Several of the commitments involved the establishment of overseas bases. This has been a primary source of tension between the executive and legislative branches, as the president asserts his authority under the commander-in-chief clause of the Constitution and the Congress sometimes resists what it perceives to be unwarranted military obligations.

As illustrated in figure 4, the number of significant military agreements has always been greater than the number of significant treaties since World War II. To estimate more precisely the extent to which significant military commitments have shifted from treaties to executive agreements, a simple Executive Agreement Index (EAI) was again constructed for each administration, based upon the proportion of significant military executive agreements among the total number of significant treaties and executive agreements (see table 17). The index has been high throughout the post–World War II era. Clearly, most of the significant military commitments between 1946 and 1973 took the form of executive agreements. Moreover, although the Eisenhower and Johnson administrations were by far the most vigorous claimants for presidential authority in this area, the other administrations were close behind.

Military agreement-making during the administration of President Gerald Ford was also tentatively examined. Of the 32 significant military commitments made overseas by the United

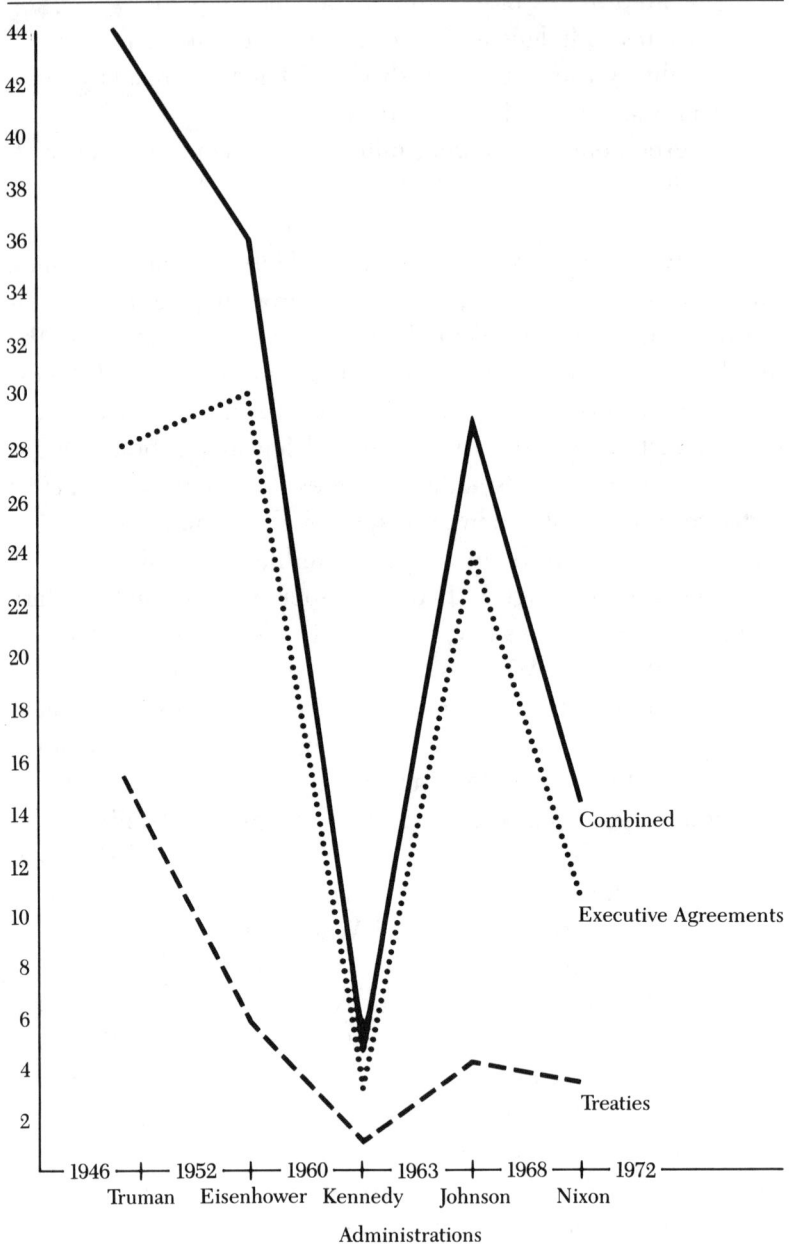

Figure 4
Number of Significant Military Treaties and Executive Agreements

The Hidden Side of Agreement-Making

States between August 9, 1974, and the end of 1976, only two were in treaty form and as many as 18 (60 percent) appeared to be executive agreements. If accurate, this figure would give the Ford administration an Executive Agreement Index of .90, slightly higher than that of the other administrations.

Military Agreements: Some Case Examples

Beyond these statistics stand a number of examples that illustrate more fully the evolution of foreign military commitments by executive fiat.

Thailand. In 1962, Secretary of State Dean Rusk and the Foreign Minister of Thailand, Thanat Khoman, issued a joint statement in which Secretary Rusk expressed "the firm intention of the United States to aid Thailand, its ally and historic trend, in resisting Communist aggression and subversion."[7] This language went far beyond that contained in the Southeast Asia Treaty Organization (SEATO) treaty, which provided only that the member nations would "consult" in times of military peril and act to meet the common danger in accordance with their own "constitutional processes."

The end result of this joint communiqué was to alter the collective security arrangement under SEATO into a bilateral U.S.–Thai defense pact. The United States Military Assistance Program (MAP) for Thailand went from $24 million in 1960 to $88 million in 1962 under the new relationship. Further, in 1966 the two nations entered into a secret joint-contingency agreement (reached in 1969), which promised joint action in the event of a conventional military attack on Thailand and paid special bonuses to Thai troops in Vietnam (in essence, the hiring of mercenaries to fight America's war). Through communiqué and secret executive agreements, the original intent of a solemn treaty was altered.[8]

Speaking more broadly than to Thailand or even Southeast

International Agreements from the Cold War to Détente

Asia alone, Secretary Rusk warned in 1966 that: "No would-be aggressor should suppose that the absence of a defense treaty, congressional declaration, or U.S. military presence grants immunity to aggression."[9] While the anti-aggressor spirit of this statement is laudable enough, its potential damage to Constitutional procedure is alarming. As Senator Frank Church (D, Idaho) noted at the time, it "put Congress on notice that, with or without its consent, treaty or no treaty, the Executive will act as it sees fit against anyone whom it judges to be an aggressor. . . . It is indeed nothing less than a statement of intention on the part of the Executive to usurp the treaty power of the Senate."[10]

Diego Garcia. A report from the General Accounting Office (GAO, an investigative arm of the Congress) uncovered that the executive branch had bypassed the Congress on the question of using Diego Garcia as a United States military base in the Indian Ocean. Through another secret agreement in 1966, the Department of State agreed to pay British costs for the evacuation of Diego Garcia to make way for American naval facilities. "We believe the method of financing—a technique which masked real plans and costs—was," concluded the report, "clearly a circumvention of the congressional oversight role."[11]

Spain. Also in the sixties, it came to light that the United States had made a series of secret agreements with Spain involving the use of Spanish soil for military bases. A covert understanding between U.S. Lt. General David Burchinal, former deputy commander of NATO, and Lt. General Manuel Diez-Alegria, former head of Spain's high general staff, committed the United States to defend Spain against third countries.[12]

The Congress as a whole remained ignorant of this arrangement for three years; a small group of its leaders, however, was well aware of the bases deal. These leaders concurred, in a meeting with Secretary of State John Foster Dulles, that it was

The Hidden Side of Agreement-Making

all right to allow executive agreements like the Spanish bases pact, since further commitments for funds were subject to the congressional appropriations process. Senator Leverett Saltonstall (R, Massachusetts) pointed out, according to Dulles, that by law actual construction of bases was subject to the approval of the Armed Services Committees.[13]

While this meeting may sound like cheery consultation between the branches, designed to ensure an institutional partnership in foreign policy-making, Senator Fulbright presents a different view. He sharply criticizes the executive branch's propensity "to tell the Chairman of the [Senate] Armed Services Committee, who usually is very sympathetic with these [executive] agreements, and the [Senate] Appropriations Committee," leaving the public and more critical legislators in the dark.[14]

As important as the question of who is told in Congress about American commitments is what occurs beyond—or in spite of—the wording on the scrap of paper that holds the agreement. In a memorandum to his Spanish counterpart, the chairman of the Joint Chiefs of Staff, General Earle Wheeler, advised in 1968 that: "By the presence of U.S. forces in Spain, the U.S. gives Spain a far more visible and credible security guarantee than any written document."[15] Just as occurred in Thailand, in Spain (concluded a Senate inquiry), "joint military planning thickened the relationship between the two countries."[16]

Disclosure of the Spanish bases executive agreement led to heated debate in the Senate Foreign Relations Committee during 1969 and 1970. "Some foreign engagements, such as our bases agreement with Spain, form a kind of quasi-commitment," said a Foreign Relations Committee report in 1969, "unspecified as to exact import but, like buds in springtime, ready, under the right climatic conditions, to burst into full bloom."[17] The critics were still a minority, though, and in 1970 Congress eventually accepted the executive agreement and authorized the funding required. The opponents of the executive agreement did manage to pass the "Church Resolution," however, in the last days of the legislative session. Sponsored by Senator Church, it resolved that "nothing in said Agreement of Friendship and Cooperation between the United States and Spain, shall be deemed to be a national commitment by the United States."[18] Boundaries were being drawn.

By the time the Spanish bases arrangement was up for renewal five yars later (1975), the insurgence in the Senate was at full tide. Prudently, the Department of State submitted the new agreement for approval as a treaty and kept key senators and staff briefed on the progress of the negotiations as they went along. According to a Senate participant, it was "a candid, open consultation",[19] and the executive branch's "tactics of accommodation" paid off with a Senate vote of 84 to 11. Ironically, Spain also aggressively sought a treaty over an executive agreement; the post-Franco regime "yearned for the symbolic benediction that a solemn treaty approved by two thirds of the Senate would provide."[20]

Ethiopia. In 1960, the United States entered into another secret pact, this time to defend Ethiopia. The Eisenhower administration pledged to support a 40,000 man Ethiopian army, promised continued military assistance, and signed a statement "reaffirming" the "continuing interest" of the United States "in the security of Ethiopia and its opposition to any activities threatening the territorial integrity of Ethiopia."[21] In exchange, the United States was allowed to construct and operate a communications station at Kagnew. Once more, the Departments of Defense and State had expanded our military commitments abroad without the knowledge of Congress or the people.

The Philippines. Like Thailand, the Philippines had established a formal military alliance with the United States based on a treaty, in this case the Philippines Mutual Defense Treaty (1952). And like the SEATO treaty, this one also promised consultation and response in accordance with constitutional processes—in other words, presumably joint actions by Congress and the presidency. Apparently, these assurances were insufficient for Philippine President Magsaysay, who requested in 1954 a firmer guarantee of American military protection.

In response, Secretary Dulles sent to Magsaysay a diplomatic note that said since our military forces were already stationed in his country "an armed attack on the Philippines could not but be also an attack upon the military forces of the United States."[22] Enter an instantaneous United States military response; exit constitutional processes. This "further bilateral assurance" (in the Department of State euphemism) was reaffirmed in 1958 by President Eisenhower and new Philippine President García through a joint communiqué, and the following year by executive agreement (the Bohlen-Serrano Agreement).[23] Today, Clark Air Force Base and the Subic Bay Naval complex in the Philippines represent the largest American bases abroad.

The stationing of American soldiers in the Philippines had been far more telling about our defense intentions than a formal treaty. As a Senate inquiry into United States military commitments abroad concluded in 1970, "overseas bases, the presence of elements of U.S. armed forces, joint planning, joint exercises, or extensive military assistance programs represent to host governments more valid assurances of U.S. commitment than any treaty or agreement."[24] The executive branch seemed more than willing to provide these assurances, without public debate on their wisdom.

South Korea. In an arrangement similar to the one struck with Thailand, the United States promised South Korea in 1966 (through secret agreement) that it would pay for commercial consumables (tires, clothing, oil products, gas) used by Korean soldiers in their homeland if Korea would send troops into combat in Vietnam. Again, the money would be quietly siphoned out of military assistance funds, supposedly appropriated for the development or purchase of new weapons.[25]

Laos. During the sixties in Laos, a wide array of secret United States military and paramilitary operations were launched without any written agreements whatsoever. Everything was based on "oral understandings" which, according to a Department of State spokesman, were just as binding as written ones.[26] Among the commitments made in this way were the absorption of three-fourths of Laos's foreign-exchange needs (including food); the loan of Agency for International Development (AID) advisers and public road experts; and the placement of American military spotters in combat zones (not to mention CIA paramilitary personnel, discussed later in this chapter). A Senate subcommittee subsequently wanted to know how this all came about:

Subcommittee Counsel: . . . under what authority are the American personnel in Laos there?
State Department spokesman: They are there under the executive authority of the President.[27]

Japan and Taiwan. Secret military agreements were negotiated with Japan and Taiwan, too. In Japan, a bombing range was constructed, astonishingly, less than three miles from public beaches, in one direction, and the Japan Atomic Fuel Corporation Laboratory, in another direction.[28] In the Republic of China (Taiwan), American military aid remained at high levels despite official reductions. The reason: agreements transferring excess military equipment to Taiwan. The obscure defense-repair program was also used to extend runways in Taiwan to handle long-range B-52 bombers destined for Vietnam.[29]

From this partial list, several lessons emerge. First, American military commitments abroad have often been based on the most slender reeds. While the oral understandings with Laos may represent an extreme example, the various secret letters, communiqués, and other agreements in these cases also exemplify a foreign policy dominated by hidden bureaucrats, closed

The Hidden Side of Agreement-Making

doors, and confidential covenants. One wonders what similar secret commitments, if any, have been made by the Reagan administration in El Salvador and Lebanon today.

Sometimes "agreements" can be strictly tacit. The presence of our soldiers or bases may mean more than the most elaborate and solemn parchment approved by the Congress. "Whether or not we have such a treaty with a particular country," testified Secretary of State Dean Rusk, "the presence there of a U.S. base clearly signified an interest and concern on our part with the security of that country."[30] The North Atlantic Treaty Organization (NATO) is a close illustration. The language of the NATO Treaty is ambiguous, but, everyone realizes that, with American troops stationed in NATO countries, an attack would inevitable draw in the United States. This truth makes the initial commitment of United States forces overseas a critical decision.

Occasionally, commitments are stretched far beyond the original intent—the so-called "creeping commitment."[31] This often happens as executive-branch officials seek to "fill in the details" once a broad agreement is reached. As with Dulles's interpretation of the Philippines Mutual Defense Treaty, the expansion of a relationship can be considerable. Such "auxilliary arrangements" within the framework of treaties and other international agreements take on a bewildering variety of forms. Among them: memoranda of understanding; exchange of notes; exchange of letters; technical arrangements; protocal; the *note verbale;* the *aide memoire;* agreed minutes; joint communiqués; joint military plans; military assistance; and, of course, the presence of armed forces. Particularly difficult for legislators to monitor are third-party agreements, whereby the United States makes assurances through intermediaries (as when we worked through Algeria to negotiate the release of our hostages in Iran).

Executive and statutory agreements are frequently justified

International Agreements from the Cold War to Détente

as stemming directly from a treaty. Yet how long should the authority of an old treaty be relied upon for the conduct of new foreign policy? In 1971, the Defense Department extended a defense arrangement with Portugal by executive agreement, later claiming authority under the NATO Treaty signed twenty-two years earlier. The costs involved for the United States amounted to almost $436 million, as well as another $5 million in drawing rights on nonmilitary excess equipment in Pentagon storage.[32] Incensed by this apparent attempt to skirt a congressional debate on United States policy toward Portugal, Clifford Case— one of the leading Senate insurgents—brought legislation to stop the flow of United States funds to Portugal in the foreign aid bill until the executive branch dealt with this matter in treaty form. Case's efforts failed in 1972 by a vote of 59 to 30, but succeeded the following year—only to see the House reject the proposed halt in foreign aid.[33]

These shell games, where Congress and the public are kept guessing about the true nature of our commitments overseas, occur in other policy areas besides the military. Secret agreements and other methods for bypassing the Congress have been used by the executive branch to conduct diplomacy, as illustrated by the Paris accord, the Sinai support mission, and the Helsinki accord.

Diplomatic Agreements

The Paris Accord

On January 27, 1973, a cease-fire agreement was reached in Paris among Vietnam War combatants. To secure a negotiated settlement, President Nixon had sent a secret message to Pham Van Dong, premier of North Vietnam, promising postwar reconstruction aid in return for his support for the peace pact. The executive branch failed to disclose the text of the

The Hidden Side of Agreement-Making

message to Congress or the public until four years later, on May 19, 1977.[34]

President Nixon also apparently made assurances to South Vietnamese President Nguyen Van Thieu, in secret letters sent in 1972 and 1973, that he intended "to take swift and severe retaliatory action" (November 14, 1972) if North Vietnam violated a cease-fire, and that we would "respond with full force should the [Paris peace] settlement be violated by North Vietnam . . ." (January 5, 1972).[35] Evidently, Saigon's signature for the peace pact was obtainable only through such open-ended promises. Again, the executive branch never informed the Congress of these letters, claiming that the communications merely represented "a statement of personal Presidential intent," not an executive agreement[36]—a collection of "private exchanges," in the words of the President's press secretary.[37] Certainly the Vietnamese took these assurances as solemn commitments, even if the President did not.[38]

The Case-Church Act, passed on August 15, 1973, to ban further use of American forces in combat throughout Indochina, stood in direct contradiction to the secret policy of the Nixon-Thieu letters. "It surpasses understanding," said Case, that the Nixon administration had failed to inform Congress that this legislation would, in effect, "nullify the commitments" in the Nixon-Thieu letters.[39]

The Sinai Support Mission

Secretary of State Henry Kissinger has been widely criticized for his use of secret agreements. Chiding him for "obsessive secrecy" in the conduct of American diplomacy, the late Senator Henry Jackson (D, Washington) once accused him of withholding from Congress for two years secret "understandings" reached with the Soviet Union during the initial nuclear strategic arms limitations talks (SALT I). Further, Kissinger apparently withheld "crucial communications" on the faltering U.S.–Soviet trade negotiations in 1974.[40] Experienced diplomatic correspondent Tad Szulc concurs in this opinion: "The fact is that virtually nobody—possibly not even Richard Nixon and Gerald Ford—knew precisely what promises and commitments Kissinger made to foreign leaders during his eight years in power: to Mao Tse-tung and Chou En-lai, Brezhnev and Dobryin, Le Duc Tho, Sadat and King Faisal, Golda Meir or any number of other foreign presidents, foreign ministers and ambassadors."[41]

One of the controversial "understandings" reached by Kissinger was with Israel and Egypt in 1975 over the question of a Sinai disengagement, which included the commitment of American personnel to serve as monitors in a region where military hostilities might have easily resumed with little warning. The "understanding" was declared by the Department of State to be the proper exercise of executive powers, not a commitment appropriate for review by the treaty procedure (although President Ford eventually sought and obtained congressional authority to implement the provisions of the accord—see chapter 6).

The Helsinki Accord

In August 1975, the Helsinki accord was signed, guaranteeing noninterference with existing boundaries in Europe and a freer flow of people and information between East and West. This declaration was sent to the Congress as a matter of "courtesy," but was never specifically reported to Congress. The Department of State reasoned that the accord was not a genuine international agreement, but only a "political statement of intent."[42] In public hearings on March 29, 1977, members of the Senate Foreign Relations Committee made it clear that they believed the Helsinki agreement should have been sent to them.

In short, efforts to circumvent the Congress on diplomatic issues have been successful, too. Interviews with legislators sug-

The Hidden Side of Agreement-Making

gest still another area where they feel the executive branch has failed in its responsibilities to keep Congress informed: intelligence policy.

Secret Intelligence Commitments

To understand the breadth of agreement-making in the intelligence field, one must begin with an overview of the mandate given the intelligence agencies in our government. These agencies are expected first of all to collect and analyze information touching on the security of the United States. The core intelligence agency, the Central Intelligence Agency (CIA, whose Director is also the coordinator—at least titularly—for the entire intelligence establishment) was, in fact, created in 1947 with one preeminent objective: to prevent another surprise attack like the one that shook the nation at Pearl Harbor.

"For ye shall know the truth and the truth shall make you free," reads the biblical injunction carved in white marble at the entrance to the CIA, chosen by Director Allen Dulles perhaps to remind his coworkers that the pursuit of objective intelligence is their *raison dêtre*. To accomplish this purpose, intelligence officers must meet the standards set by Sherman Kent, the top CIA analyst for many years. He emphasized the importance of "the best in professional training, the highest intellectual integrity, and a very large amount of worldly wisdom."[43] This in itself, however, is insufficient; the analyst must have facts, opinions, and even speculations from around the globe. The quest for raw data depends upon classic and modern forms of espionage (from the spy with two legs to the spy-in-the-sky with a hundred lenses), as well as secret agreements with other nations to share intelligence personnel, equipment, and information.[44]

Our need for information about a dangerous global environment, then, propels us toward covert agreement-making with

International Agreements from the Cold War to Détente

allies. For the most part, these arrangements are vital for the national defense. A problem arises, though, when the agreements involve questionable methods, dubious partnerships, and dangerous risks. Inevitably, as with all agreement-making, the acceptable degree of executive discretion in these matters must be determined. As things have stood for most of the history of the CIA and other intelligence agencies, the degree of discretion has been almost total when it came to intelligence agreements abroad.[45] This includes agreements for both intelligence collection and a second major area of responsibility for the intelligence community: counterintelligence, the effort to thwart hostile intelligence services and internal subversives.

Which agents or (more likely) what gathered intelligence should be shared with, say, British intelligence; what surveillance equipment (a U-2 reconnaissance plane, for instance) should be loaned to a friendly Third World nation with a war-prone neighbor on its borders; or, to turn from intelligence collection to counterintelligence, what range of antiterrorist techniques should be taught to a Latin American junta plagued by guerilla bombings? In each of these instances, United States intelligence agencies might decide to enter into covert agreements with foreign powers. The questions of control are self-evident. Among them: How well are such agreements coordinated within the executive branch? Do they comport with State Department policy? Should they require National Security Council (NSC) or presidential approval? Are they, or should they, be reported to Congress? Should they require congressional approval?

These questions apply to the third major area of intelligence responsibility, too: the controversial policy of "covert action" (CA), defined by the CIA as any program designed to influence events abroad covertly in support of U.S. foreign and national security policies. A more comprehensive definition of covert action is found in Executive Order 12036 on "United States Intelligence Activities," issued during the Carter administration.

The Hidden Side of Agreement-Making

Referring to CAs as "special activities," the Executive Order states:

Special activities means activities conducted abroad in support of national foreign policy objectives which are designed to further official United States programs and policies abroad and which are planned and executed so that the role of the United States Government is not apparent or acknowledged publicly, and functions in support of such activities, but not including diplomatic activity or the collection and production of intelligence or related support functions (Sec. 4-212).

As far as the Congress is concerned, the most relevant formal definition of covert action was established in the language of the Hughes-Ryan Amendment to the Foreign Assistance Act (passed in December 1974).[46] This law defines covert action as CIA "operations in foreign countries, other than activities intended solely for obtaining necessary intelligence." In practice, this definition has become the governing concept for government officials.

In a word, then, CA is secret activity to influence events abroad. This objective is pursued through a wide array of political means and varying degrees of force. Traditionally, CA techniques are grouped into four broad categories: paramilitary, political action, economic action, and propaganda. (The last three categories are sometimes combined into one, called "political action.")

The nation's first covert action apparently took place as long ago as the early 1800s. According to historian Robert Wallace:

In Washington, Eaton, the U.S. Consul in Tunis, laid before Jefferson a scheme that had been developing among Americans in the Mediterranean for a couple of years. The Bashaw of Tripoli was a usurper, having stolen the throne from an older brother who was now wandering forlornly somewhere in Africa. Eaton proposed to find the brother, give him sympathy and support, and install him as rightful head of state. Jefferson approved the idea and thus was launched the first, although not the last, American effort to overthrow an objectionable foreign ruler and put a cooperative one in his place. Jefferson also chose to have that plot proceed quietly, in twilight. He would send the would-be Bashaw, through Eaton, a few artillery pieces and 1,000 small arms. Eaton himself was to be given a vague title—'Navy agent of the United States for Barbary regencies'—and placed under the jurisdiction of the commodore of the Mediterranean squadron. If he could accomplish something, fine. If not, small loss.[47]

As with the would-be Bashaw, CA operations often involve the reaching of a secret agreement of one kind or another in which American resources or personnel are committed to foreign officials or their adversaries. Though not traditionally thought of in this light, intelligence pacts involving collaboration in collection, counterintelligence, or covert-action operations represent still another (quite hidden) form of international agreement-making. The range of CA operations is sweeping, and often highly risky, drawing for their authority in the modern era on a catch-all phrase of the 1947 National Security Act that created the CIA. This phrase directs the CIA to "perform such other functions and duties related to intelligence affecting the national security as the National Security Council may from time to time direct" (50 U.S.C. 403).

Some examples, past and present, serve to illustrate the scope of operations that have been enclosed within the circle of covert action since 1947—all leading to agreements struck with countries or factions abroad.

Paramilitary (PM). Paramilitary, or warlike, operations have always been the riskiest covert actions. These operations may consist of support to groups engaged in insurgency fighting; the funding of paramilitary training activities (including counterterrorist training); the dispatch of CIA military advisers; and the direct or indirect shipment of arms, ammunition, or other military equipment abroad.

In the conduct of PM missions, secret agreements for covert cooperation have been reached with Ukranian guerrillas (1949–

The Hidden Side of Agreement-Making

53); Polish resistance groups (1950–52); Albanian rebels (1949–52); Tibetan insurgents (1953–59); splinter groups in Mainland China and North Korea (1950–54); and factions in Guatemala (1954), in Cuba (1961–64), in Laos (throughout the sixties), and in Vietnam (1955–74), to provide only a partial list.[48] Assassination of foreign leaders represents one form of PM. While plotting the death of selected foreign leaders, the CIA entered into secret pacts with dissident factions in a number of small countries, according to a Senate investigation in 1975.[49]

For Castro dissidents, the Agency prepared a cache composed of "a rifle with a scope and silencer, plus several bombs, concealed either in a suitcase or some other concealment" which an agent could carry and place next to the Cuban premier. For Trujillo dissidents, the CIA was prepared to air-drop twelve "sterile" (that is, untraceable) rifles with telescopic sights into the Dominican Republic. The drop was never made, since the rebels postponed their plans for a coup. Later, various dissident groups requested sundry weapons from CIA agents. In March 1961, for instance, a request was passed for fifty fragmentation grenades, five rapid-fire weapons, and ten 64mm antitank rockets. Through Department of State channels traveled information about the dissidents and their requests, disguised with references to a picnic: ". . . the members of our club [i.e., dissidents] are now prepared in their minds to have a picnic [coup]. Lately they have developed a plan for the picnic, which just might work if they could find the proper food [weapons]. They have asked us for a few sandwiches [guns]. . . . Last week we were asked to furnish three or four pineapples [fragmentation grenades] for a picnic in the near future. . . ."[50] Eventually, three .38 caliber pistols were sent to the CIA station chief in the Dominican Republic, using a diplomatic pouch, and these "sandwiches" were then passed on to dissidents. Later, three .30 caliber M1 carbines stored in the United States Consulate were also given to the dissidents. To opponents of the Allende regime in Chile, the United States passed three .45 caliber submachine guns, six tear-gas grenades, and five hundred rounds of ammunition in October 1970.[51] Various other United States–supplied weapons went to opponents of President Sukarno of Indonesia and Duvalier of Haiti.[52]

Political action. The political action side of covert action includes sundry sub rosa relationships with influential foreign personalities (so-called agents of influence), operations to manipulate foreign economies, and deception and propaganda programs in support of American foreign policy. Here American intelligence agencies have entered into secret agreements over the years with the pro-Western Christian Democratic Party in Italy; pro-Western factions in Greece, West Germany, and the Philippines (consistently during the Cold War); and pro-Western groups in Iran (1951–53), Ecuador (1959–63), and Chile (1958–73).[53]

In Chile, the United States secretly spent over $13 million in opposition to President Salvador Allende. In the 1964 Chilean election alone, the CIA spent $3 million. Comparing our population with Chile's, this $3 million would amount to about $60 million in an American presidential election. (In the 1964 presidential campaign, President Johnson and Senator Barry Goldwater, his opponent, combined spent $25 million).[54]

Until 1974 (see chapter 5), none of these paramilitary and political action operations had to be revealed to members of Congress; few were. As Allen Dulles once told a colleague, "I'll tell the truth to Dick [Richard B. Russell, chairman of the Senate oversight subcommittee on the CIA]. I always do. That is, if Dick wants to know."[55] Senator Russell (D, Georgia) rarely wanted to know.[56] He apparently felt the same way as his Southern colleague John Stennis (D, Mississippi), who succeeded him as top CIA overseer in the Senate. "You have to make up your mind that you are going to have an intelligence agency," said Stennis, "and protect it as such and shut your eyes

The Hidden Side of Agreement-Making

and take what is coming."[57] The end result of this head-in-the-sand approach to foreign policy was a steady flow of secret intelligence commitments abroad, largely unmonitored by elected representatives of the American people.

Too often the executive branch has bypassed the Congress to make major foreign commitments simply by signing an executive agreement, writing a letter, or making a promise. The Congress has long been aware of this practice, but—until recently—its efforts to correct matters have met with little success. At a Senate Foreign Relations Committee hearing in 1971, Senator Fulbright noted that "we have discovered that the President does not always know best, and that, indeed, the country would be far better off today if the Congress had been more assertive in the exercise of its constitutional role, which consists as least as much in assertion and criticism as it does in subservience."[58] The legislative response to executive discretion in agreement-making is the subject of the second part of this book.

Notes

1. "Transmittal of Executive Agreements to Congress," Senate Report No. 92-591, 92nd Cong., 2nd Sess., January 19, 1972, pp. 3-4.

2. See "Making Foreign Policy Through International Agreement," in Francis O. Wilcox and Richard A. Frank, eds., *The Constitution and the Conduct of Foreign Policy* (New York: Praeger, 1976), p. 128.

3. *Congressional Record*, 95th Cong., 2nd Sess., June 28, 1978, p. S9996.

4. See "Transmittal of Executive Agreements to Congress," *Hearings*, Senate Foreign Relations Committee, 92nd Cong., 1st Sess., October 20 and 21, 1971, p. 2.

5. "Congressional Oversight of Executive Agreements," *Hearings*, Subcommittee on Separation of Powers, Senate Judiciary Committee, 92nd Cong., 2nd Sess., April 24, 25, May 12, 18, 19, 1972, p. 54.

6. "Executive Agreements with Portugal and Bahrain," *Hearings*, Senate Foreign Relations Committee, 92nd Cong., 2nd Sess., February 1, 2, 3, 1972, p. 4.

7. See "National Commitments," Report No. 91-129, Senate Committee on Foreign Relations, 91st Cong., 1st Sess. (April 16, 1969), p. 28. See also

International Agreements from the Cold War to Détente

Frank Church, "Of Presidents and Caesars: The Decline of Constitutional Government in the Conduct of American Foreign Policy," *Idaho Law Review* v 6 (Fall 1969).

8. See "U.S. Security Agreements and Commitments Abroad: Laos and Thailand," *Hearings,* Subcommittee on United States Security Agreements and Commitments Abroad, Senate Foreign Relations Committee, Part 6, 1969–1970, hereafter cited as the Symington Subcommittee (after its Chairman, Stuart Symington, D, Missouri).

9. "Worldwide Military Commitments," *Hearings,* Subcommittee on Preparedness, Senate Armed Services Committee, 89th Cong., 2d. Sess., August 25, 1966, p. 9.

10. Church, op. cit., p. 4.

11. See the *Washington Post,* January 25, 1975.

12. See the *Washington Post,* October 14, 1976.

13. Letter from Dulles to William Knowland (R, California), the Senate Majority Leader, July 23, 1953, printed in "Spain and Portugal," *Hearings,* the Symington Subcommittee, op. cit., Part 11, p. 433.

14. "Morocco and Libya," *Hearings,* Symington Subcommittee, Part 9, ibid., p. 1979.

15. Memorandum to Gen. Diez-Alegria, November 18, 1968, printed in "Spain and Portugal," *Hearings,* op. cit., p. 2356.

16. Ibid., p. 52.

17. "National Commitments" Report, op. cit., p. 28.

18. *Congressional Record,* December 11, 1970, p. 41167.

19. J. Brian Atwood, "Downtown Perspective: Lessons on Liaison with Congress," in Thomas M. Franck, ed., *The Tethered Presidency* (New York: New York University Press, 1981), p. 217. Atwood served as an aide to Senator Thomas Eagleton (D, Missouri) at the time.

20. Ibid., p. 218.

21. "Ethiopia," *Hearings,* Symington Subcommittee, Part 8, p. 1904–05.

22. Senate Foreign Relations Committee Report, December 21, 1970, p. 5.

23. *New York Times,* April 9, 1954, p. 2. By 1983, the United States was spending close to $1 billion in aid to the Philippines for the privilege of a further five-year lease for American bases there. Philippine President Ferdinand E. Marcos's favor was curried with more than cash; in 1981, Vice President George Bush praised Marcos's support for "democracy," stretching that word to the breaking point, and President Reagan offered an enthusiastic welcome to the Philippine President on his state visit to the United States in 1982. See Bernard Gwertzman, "For U.S., Global Needs Can Overshadow Human Rights," *New York Times* August 28, 1983, p. 1E.

24. Senate Foreign Relations Committee Report, December 21, 1970, p. 20.

The Hidden Side of Agreement-Making

25. Ibid., p. 9.
26. "Kingdom of Laos," *Hearings,* Symington Subcommittee, Part 2, p. 437.
27. Ibid., p. 433.
28. "Japan," *Hearings,* ibid., Part 8.
29. "Republic of China," *Hearings,* ibid., Part 7.
30. *Hearings,* Subcommittee on Preparedness, Senate Committee on Armed Services, August 25, 1966, p. 4.
31. This phrase is from a Senate Foreign Relations Committee Report, December 21, 1970, p. 4.
32. "Agreements with Portugal and Bahrain," Senate Foreign Relations Committee Report (No. 92–632), 1972, p. 3.
33. See the *Congressional Record,* June 28, 1972, p. 22904, and, in 1973, pp. 12627, 29235, and 33577.
34. See the *Washington Post,* June 2, 1977. The letter was dated February 1, 1973.
35. See the *Washington Post,* May 6, 1975; also, April 9 and April 10, 1975. See, too, Gareth Porter, "The Broken Promise to Hanoi," *The Nation,* April 30, 1977, pp. 519–521; and Leslie H. Gelb, "A Domestic Challenge to Executive Agreements," *New York Times,* August 17, 1975.
36. Gelb, ibid. On the use of financial "bribes" to seal agreements, see the remarks of strategic arms negotiator, Paul C. Warnke, summarized by Vernon A. Guidry Jr., "Warnke Hits SALT 'Bribes,' " *Washington Star,* December 6, 1978.
37. *Washington Post,* April 10, 1975.
38. Ibid., June 2, 1977.
39. Ibid., May 6, 1975.
40. Ibid., April 9, 1975.
41. *The Illusion of Peace* (New York: Viking, 1979), p. 212.
42. Author's telephone conversation with Arthur W. Rovine, Office of the Legal Adviser for Treaty Affairs, Department of State, March 29, 1977.
43. *Strategic Intelligence for World Policy* (Princeton, Princeton University Press, 1949, 1966), pp. 64–65.
44. On the issue of secret intelligence agreements, see Gordon B. Baldwin, "Congressional Power to Demand Disclosure of Foreign Intelligence Agreements," *Brooklyn Journal of International Law* 3 (1976), pp. 1–30. One published example is the presence of five American intelligence bases in Turkey, used for seismic monitoring of Soviet nuclear explosions, missile tracking, and naval movements in the Black Sea. These bases cost the United States $1 billion for a four-year lease. See the *New York Times,* May 15, 1977, p. 14.
45. In 1976, a Senate investigative committee concluded that American intelligence agreements with the intelligence services of foreign powers "have not been systematically reviewed by the Congress in any fashion." "Foreign

and Military Intelligence," Senate Select Committee to Study Governmental Operations with Respect to Intelligence Activities (the Church Committee), Final Report, Book I, Senate Report No. 94–755, 94 Cong., 1st Sess., April 26, 1976, p. 459.

46. Also known as Section 662(a) of the 1974 Foreign Assistance Act, the Amendment was sponsored by Senator Harold E. Hughes (D, Iowa) and Representative Leo J. Ryan (D, California). This Act was amended in 1980, but the earlier definition of covert action is still used by officials.

47. "The Barbary Wars" *Smithsonian* (January 1975), p. 21.

48. On covert action, see Harry Rositzke, *CIA's Secret Operations: Espionage, Counter Espionage, and Covert Action* (New York: Reader's Digest, 1977); and Victor Marchetti and John D. Marks, *The CIA and the Cult of Intelligence* (New York: Knopf, 1974).

49. See "Alleged Assassination Plots Involving Foreign Leaders," the Senate Select Committee on Intelligence (the Church Committee), Report No. 94–465, 94th Cong., 1st Sess., November 20, 1975, from which the following examples are drawn.

50. Ibid., p. 199.

51. Ibid., pp. 243–44.

52. Ibid., p. 4, note 1.

53. See Rositzke and Marchetti and Marks, op. cit. On Chile see "Covert Action," *Hearings*, Senate Select Committee to Study Governmental Operations with Respect to Intelligence Activities (the Church Committee), 94th Cong., 1st Sess. December 4 and 5, 1975.

54. See "Covert Action," *Hearings*, ibid., p. 10.

55. Tom Braden, "CIA: Power and Arrogance," *Washington Post*, April 27, 1975.

56. See Jerrold L. Walden, "The CIA: A Study in the Arrogation of Administrative Powers," *The George Washington Law Review* 39 (October, 1970) 66–101, for an indication of how infrequently CIA representatives met with their legislative overseers.

57. Quoted by Harry Howe Ransom, "The Uses (and Abuses) of Secret Power," *Worldview* 18 (May 1975): 11–15.

58. "Transmittal of Executive Agreements," 1972, op. cit., p. 3.

II.

The Democratic Control of International Agreements

4.

The Bricker Revolt

> The primary purpose of [the Resolution] is to prohibit the use of the treaty as an instrument of domestic legislation for surrendering national sovereignty.
>
> —SENATOR JOHN BRICKER, *Hearing,* MAY 21, 1952

Insurgence

During the postwar period, Congress engaged in two major attempts to curb executive discretion in the commitment of the United States abroad. The first occurred in the fifties and was unsuccessful. Led by Senator John W. Bricker (R. Ohio), legislators in the Senate sought to amend the Constitution in such a way as to limit sharply the president's authority to make international agreements and the effect of such agreements on American domestic law.

The second attempt occurred in the seventies and was partially successful. Led by legislators in the Senate and the House wary of executive excesses during the Vietnam War, this initiative had (at first) the modest goal of requiring the executive branch to inform Congress of foreign pacts entered into by this country. Subsequent efforts were made, however, to go beyond the establishment of simple reporting requirements toward greater legislative control over agreement-making. These efforts ran aground.

This chapter reviews the Bricker revolt; the following chapter explores the insurgence against presidential power led by opponents of the Vietnam War. The Brickerites and the Vietnam "doves" were worlds apart in ideology and separated by almost two decades, but wedded historically in their distrust of executive power.

The Brickerites

Among the most controversial proposals considered by Congress during the early years of the Cold War were those introduced by Senator Bricker to amend the treaty clauses of the Constitution. Chairman of the Foreign and Interstate Commerce Committee during the fifties, Bricker had won successive elections in Ohio—first as attorney general, three times as governor, and twice as United States Senator. In 1944, he had been his party's vice-presidential nominee. In the Senate, Bricker identified with the conservative wing of the Republican party; he opposed government controls on business and usually voted for budget cuts. On foreign policy he seemed ambivalent, voting for NATO and the Marshall Plan, but repeatedly opposing other foreign assistance to Europe.[1]

Most troubling to Senator Bricker and his supporters was Article VI, Clause 2 of the Constitution, which reads: "This Constitution, and the Laws of the United States which shall be made in Pursuance thereof; and all Treaties made, or which shall be made, under the Authority of the United States, shall be the supreme Law of the Land; and the Judges in every State shall be bound thereby, any Thing in the Constitution or Laws of any State to the Contrary notwithstanding." To the Brickerites,

The Bricker Revolt

this passage allowed the president, in effect, to add to the Constitutional system by making treaties and other agreements "under the authority of the United States," which would, in turn, bind state and federal law. By international agreement, the president or his subordinates might impose upon the nation legal obligations that would invade the domain of power reserved to the states and, thereby, deprive the people of rights guaranteed under the Constitution. The Bricker movement, in a nutshell, was a thinly disguised defense of states' rights, a concept dear to the conservative wings of both major parties,

Some credence to this view was warranted, because the Supreme Court had earlier rendered two important decisions that gave wide executive discretion in agreement-making, nullifying state statute and state control. One, *Missouri v. Holland* (252 U.S. 416, 1920), strengthened the treaty power of the president, while the other, *U.S. v. Pink* (315 U.S. 203, 1942), legitimized the executive-agreement power of the president based on Article VI and voided state statute.

Missouri v. Holland addressed the validity of a congressional act (the Migratory Bird Treaty Act of 1918) passed to implement a treaty between the United States and Great Britain. The treaty sought the establishment of closed shooting seasons in Canada and the United States. The state of Missouri brought an action to enjoin federal game warden Holland from enforcing the law, arguing before the Court that this act was void. The Constitution did not delegate this power to the Congress, reasoned Missouri and, as a result, the regulation of migratory birds was reserved to the states by the Tenth Amendment. In fact, in two earlier cases—prior to the signing of the treaty—a similar act of Congress was held improper by federal courts in Arkansas and Kansas.

Justice Oliver Wendell Holmes, however, disagreed with these precedents in his opinion for the majority: "Acts of Congress are the supreme law of the land only when made in pursuance of the Constitution, while treaties are declared to be so when made under the authority of the United States. . . . It is obvious that there may be matters of the sharpest exigency for the national well-being that an act of Congress could not deal with but that a treaty followed by such an act could. . . ."[2] Justice Holmes argued that migratory birds were transitory inhabitants of the states, and the federal government was best left to regulate their well-being. Moreover, he said, even though the Constitution was silent on this issue, such grounds were not sufficient to support the claim by the state of Missouri and, further, "a treaty may override its power."[3] In effect, then, and what disturbed the Brickerites so much, the Court concluded that the treaty power could override the rights of the states.

The second case, *Pink*, involved the federal government's claim to the assets of the First Russian Insurance Company, which were held as a security for doing business in the state by the New York Superintendent of Insurance (Mr. Pink). Following the 1917 Revolution, Russia nationalized the Insurance Company and claimed title to its assets. In turn, the United States based its claim to the assets upon the Hull-Litvinov Agreement—an executive agreement that established diplomatic relations with the Soviet Union and assigned the remaining Russian assets in the United States to the federal government. While the New York Court of Appeals dismissed the complaint and said that the laws of the state of New York should apply to this company, the Supreme Court agreed to hear an appeal. Justice William O. Douglas wrote the opinion for the majority and upheld the federal government's claim to the assets. The legitimacy of the Litvinov Agreement, and its supremacy over state law, was the basis of the judgment. As Justice Douglas wrote: "A treaty is 'Law of the Land' under the supremacy clause (Art. VI, cl. 2) of the Constitution. Such international compacts and agreements as the Litvinov Agreement have a similar dignity."[4] In short, executive agreements, too, were another in-

The Bricker Revolt

strument for the federal government to exercise control over the affairs of the states—a second serious challenge to states' rights, as well as a further vehicle available to the president for involving the United States with governments abroad.

A third important court decision, and one more proximate to the time of the Bricker controversy, highlighted an immediate concern about the treaty powers: the perceived dangers from the United Nations Charter and its myriad treaty proposals. (In contrast to the earlier cases, this one was at the state level; however, the results for the Bricker advocates were as equally disturbing as the *Missouri* and *Pink* cases.) In this case, *Fujii v. California* (217p. 2d 481), the California Court of Appeals overturned the California Alien Land Act on grounds that it was in conflict with the Charter of the United Nations: since the United States had signed the UN Charter (a treaty) in 1945, the government was bound by it.[5] This decision allowed Fujii, a Japanese national ineligible for American citizenship, to own land in California despite a state law to the contrary. Although the decision was later overturned by the California Supreme Court, the implications for the Bricker supporters were all too clear: the UN treaty (and all treaties) could produce foreign interference in the exercise of American rights, including the rights of states. The case drew a sharp reaction from Senator Bricker when he introduced his first constitutional amendment in 1952. "In my judgment," said Bricker, "the decision of the California court in the *Fujii* case was wrong . . . if the principle announced therein should be sustained, literally thousands of Federal and State laws will automatically become invalid. . . . Obviously something must be done to prevent treaties from having such far-reaching and unintended consequences."[6]

Also disturbing to Brickerites were proposals before the United Nations to advance an antigenocide convention, a declaration of human rights, and other proposals, which, if adopted as treaties by the United States, would have pledged—so feared the

Brickerites—this country to endless interference in the domestic affairs of other countries and, perhaps more importantly, invited their interference in ours. Here was a paramount concern. According to one student of the Bricker era, many Southern senators dreaded that the federal government might declare desegregation in the United States by means of an executive agreement, perhaps with an African ally.[7]

As early as 1943, New Dealer devotion to the idea of a United Nations had already inflamed passions among conservative critics on Capitol Hill—especially the instrument of commitment preferred by the Department of State. With reference to a United Nations Relief and Rehabilitation Administration (UNRRA) draft agreement, the State Department informed influential anti–New Dealer Arthur Vandenberg, Republican Senator from Michigan, that "the United States participation in the establishment of this United Nations administration should be through an executive agreement."[8]

Vandenberg wasted no time in reply. The draft, he said, "pledged our total resources to whatever illimitable scheme for relief and rehabilitation all around the world our New Deal crystal gazers might desire to pursue . . . [with] no interference with this world-wide prospectus as it might be conceived by Roosevelt, Lehman, Hopkins and Co., until that long last moment when Congress would be confronted with a 'fait accompli.' "[9] The State Department abandoned its talk of an executive agreement, but signed one anyhow (only later converted into a statutory agreement through authorizing legislation).[10]

Behind the ardent defense of states' rights and the distaste for New Dealers stood another danger perceived by the Brickerites: secret executive agreements. The memory of President Roosevelt's secret agreements with the Soviets during World War II—the bugaboo of the Republican Party since the end of the War—remained a central concern of the Bricker forces. The

The Bricker Revolt

Wisconsin State Republican party, for instance, in its 1953 censure of Senator Alexander Wiley (R, Wisconsin), then Chairman of the Foreign Relations Committee and a foe of the Bricker Amendment, resolved: "The power of executive agreements has resulted in such catastrophes as Yalta, Potsdam, and Tehran . . . the Bricker amendment is designed to safeguard our freedoms."[11]

Stirrings in the Senate

Efforts to allay such concerns by means of a Constitutional amendment began early in the fifties. In contrast to the seventies, when both the House and the Senate were involved in challenging the executive, the focal point in the fifties was the United States Senate. On September 14, 1951, Senator Bricker introduced Senate Joint Resolution (S.J. Res.) 102, which would have replaced the second clause in Article VI of the Constitution.[12] This resolution was referred to the Committee on the Judiciary. It received no further attention in that session of the Congress, but the congressional-executive struggle had been joined.

The next year Senator Bricker once against introduced a Constitutional amendment, S.J. Res. 130.[13] The resolution was referred to the Committee on the Judiciary, and, this time, public hearings were held in May and June.[14] Congress adjourned in July 1952, however, without further action on the proposed amendment. Each of these early versions of the Bricker Amendment sought to prevent the use of treaties or executive agreements to abridge the Constitutional or states' rights of American citizens, or to vest in an international organization any rights belonging to American citizens. Further, S.J. Res. 130 also stated explicitly in section 4 that "[e]xecutive agreements shall not be made in lieu of treaties."

During the May 21 hearings, Senator Bricker expressed the

views of many senators with this testimony in support of his amendment: "The issues are fundamental. They concern the sovereignty and the Constitution of the United States. . . . The necessity for this Amendment is shown by the activities of the United Nations and certain of its specialized agencies. There is practically no human activity which treaties now under consideration by the U.N. do not seek to regulate."[15]

On January 7, 1953, Senator Bricker once more placed his resolution (now S.J. Res. 1) into the Senate's in basket. This resolution was eventually signed by 62 cosponsors from the Senate membership.[16] Its resemblance to the earlier amendments was close, though Bricker toned down his frontal attack on all executive agreements. ("All executive or other agreements . . . shall be made only in the manner and the extent to be prescribed by law.") If in conformity with existing law ("statutory agreements," in the language of this study), executive agreements seemed to be acceptable; "pure" or unilateral executive agreements of the FDR destroyers-for-bases variety were, however, strictly forbidden.

The resolution was again referred to the Committee on the Judiciary, which held public hearings in February, March, and April.[17] During the hearings, the Eisenhower administration rolled out its heavy artillery in opposition to the proposal. Secretary of State John Foster Dulles, Attorney General Herbert Brownell, and various other high-ranking officials (including Frank Nash, Assistant Secretary of Defense, and Harold Stassen, Director for Mutual Security) spoke against the amendment and its potential hindrance in the operations of their departments. In a press conference, President Eisenhower, too, said that the amendment was "unnecessary and dangerous," although he failed to make the administration's case clear and forcefully.[18]

Interest groups also lined up for and against the Bricker Amendment. The President's backers included the American Federation of Labor, the League of Women Voters, the

The Bricker Revolt

American Veterans' Committee, Erwin Griswold, Dean of the Harvard Law School, and the well-known authority on the presidency, Edward S. Corwin. Among Bricker's supporters were the Committee on Peace and Law of the American Bar Association, the Vigilant Women for the Bricker Amendment, the American Medical Association, the American Legion, the Daughters of the American Revolution, the Veterans of Foreign Wars, Kiwanis International, the American Farm Bureau Federation, and the Chamber of Commerce of the United States—a formidable listing by any reckoning.[19]

On June 15, 1953, S.J. Res. 1 was sent to the Senate floor by a favorable vote of the Judiciary Committee.[20] Pulling and hauling, accommodation and compromise, had led to modification in the original language—an inevitable by-product of subcommittee and committee mark-up. The new, somewhat weakened wording, still bore strong teeth in its key sections:

Sec. 1. A provision of a treaty which conflicts with this Constitution shall not be of any force or effect.
Sec. 2. A treaty shall become effective as internal law in the United States only through legislation *which would be valid in the absence of treaty* (emphasis added).
Sec. 3. Congress shall have power to regulate all executive agreements and other agreements with any foreign power or international organization. All such arguments shall be subject to the limitations imposed on treaties by this article.

The ambiguities were evident. What, for instance, did the Committee mean by "regulate" in Section 3? Did the "other agreements" in Section 3 include informal commitments? Such questions would consume many days of debate in the Senate during 1953 and 1954.

The Issues

While various versions of the Bricker Amendment were presented to the Senate in the fifties, S.J. Res. 1 was the heart of the revolt in 1953–1954 and embraced the key issues surrounding the ongoing tug of war. For this reason, this particular resolution is analyzed in detail below. The principal sources of information on the resolution are the hearings,[21] Senate Report No. 412,[22] the formal debate in the Senate in 1953 and 1954,[23] and the various scholarly commentaries.[24]

Section 1

Pro. Proponents of the Bricker Amendment argued that Section 1 was necessary because "[i]t would, for example, prevent the UN Human Rights convenants and other dangerous UN treaties from authorizing what the Constitution expressly forbids."[25] Such international covenants would void or abridge the civil liberties of Americans, argued the pro-Bricker witnesses, as well as give an international organization jurisdiction over these rights as exercised within the United States. The Executive Secretary of the Daughters of the American Revolution testified: "Our organization will continue to fight those who seek to destroy American independence for the sake of world government. We will continue to oppose those who try to indoctrinate our children with the idea that they are now world citizens or citizens of the United Nations rather than American citizens."[26]

More generally, this section ensured that all treaties would be made in conformity with the Constitution, not simply "under the authority of the United States" as provided in Article VI. No treaties that violated the Constitution could be put into effect. This "loophole" in the Constitution would be closed.[27]

Con. Representing the Administration, Attorney General Brownell conceded that in *Missouri v. Holland* Justice Holmes may have indulged in undue speculation on the authority of treaties; but, Brownell noted, Holmes qualified his opinion with this observation: "We do not mean to imply that there are no qualifications to the treaty-making power." Holmes said, moreover, that the treaty before the Court "does not contravene any prohibitory words of the Constitution." Thus, just because the Supreme Court had never declared a treaty unconstitutional did not imply that it would fail to do so in the future.[28] Protestations of the Brickerites to the contrary notwithstanding, it was settled law already that no treaty could alter or subvert the Constitution.

At the time of the hearings in 1953, historian Henry Steele Commager emphasized that the executive branch had never entered into a treaty subsequently held to be in conflict with the Constitution. In contrast, he observed, "seventy or eighty Acts of Congress have been held void by the Courts. If we are going to have amendments to prevent unconstitutional actions by branches of the national government, perhaps Senator Bricker had better start with Congress!"[29] Professor Corwin concluded simply that Section 1 "would leave things just as they stand today—it would be surplusage."[30]

Section 2

Pro. Section 2, the heart of the Amendment, was essential to the Brickerites because of Articles 55 and 56 of the UN Charter, which concern international social cooperation and human rights. Many state statutes would be automatically void, argued Senator Bricker, if these articles were to be regarded by the United States courts as self-executing. He criticized self-executing agreements as a method for achieving domestic consequences neither sanctioned nor foreseen during the original process.[31] By prohibiting self-executing treaties, and by providing that any agreement or treaty had to be accompanied by legislation valid in the absence of an agreement or treaty (that is, would not infringe on states' rights), the Brickerites sought to eliminate the legal ambiguity between domestic and international areas of responsibility on the part of the president and the Congress.

The Democratic Control of International Agreements

The upshot of this so-called "which clause" ("which would be valid in the absence of a treaty") would have been to require implementing legislation from the various state legislatures whenever matters of states' rights were at issue[32]—a staggering involvement of individual states in the making of foreign policy commitments. Even when questions of states' rights were absent, congressional implementing legislation would have been necessary to validate an international agreement.

Alfred J. Schweppe, Chairman of the Committee on Peace and Law of the American Bar Association, stated before the Judiciary subcommittee:

> The purpose of [Section 2] is to take the Trojan-horse element out of the treaty clause. Today a treaty is made. Two or three or five years from now the several States find out that while everybody was asleep, including probably Congress and the States, a provision was put into the treaty which has the effect of invalidating a State constitutional provision or a State law. That comes about by reason of the supreme-law clause in the sixth article, which makes treaties automatically domestic law. Any self-executing treaty becomes automatically domestic law once it has been ratified [sic] by the Senate of the United States, State constitutions and laws to the contrary notwithstanding.
>
> What this [Section] does is to render all treaties non–self-executing.[33]

Mr. Schweppe continued: "Without such a constitutional limitation, and within the recent State Department concept that 'there is no longer any real distinction between domestic and foreign affairs' (see *American Bar Association Journal*, September 1952, p. 737), the President and two-thirds of the Senators present could take over the entire area of internal law now reserved to the States . . . ."[34] The "which clause" was thus justified as a protection of states' rights and would have voided the doctrine embodied in *Missouri v. Holland*.

Con. The basic arguments against the "which clause" revolved around the beliefs that the Senate and the president could be trusted not to impair the rights of American citizens by trea-

The Bricker Revolt

ties or agreement;[35] that, further, the Senate could refuse approval of such treaties, attach reservations, and insist that any treaty be non–self-executing; that the Supreme Court can declare any treaty unconstitutional; and that if an objectionable treaty or agreement was approved, the Congress could override it by passing a law that would replace the international agreement.[36]

Opponents pointed out, moreover, that under Section 2 a treaty proposal would have to go through an extraordinarily cumbersome process. Even if state legislatures were not brought into the picture, added to the two steps required at present—a two-thirds vote of the senators present and ratification by the president—Section 2 would require implementing legislation by a majority vote in the House and Senate, as well as, finally, the approval of the president once again—who by that time might be a different president. As the Attorney General said, with exasperation, during the hearings: "Not only is the double step unprecedented, but it is unnecessary."[37] The Department of State echoed the criticism: "Our ability to assure those with whom we negotiated that when we seal the bargain, there is a reasonable ground to believe that it will be made effective with the advice and consent of the Senate, is an essential ingredient in our ability to negotiate successfully."[38]

The most serious flaw in Section 2 (according to the anti-Brickerites) remained, however, the possible effect of the notorious "which clause." Historian Commager, for one, emphasized that most American treaties (including the significant ones) have dealt with matters usually delegated to the states. Among his examples were numerous treaties dealing with "reciprocal rights to own property, to inherit, to do business," and the like.[39] The "which clause" would strip the United States of the "normal attributes and necessary powers of a sovereign nation," according to other testimony;[40] the international control of atomic facilities or weapons of mass destruction would be greatly hindered;[41] and, among other things, treaties for control of domestic narcotics production would be unenforceable in various aspects.[42] Concluded Professor Corwin, magisterially:

No such act of mayhem on the Constitution is required to meet existing perils. The Anti-Genocide Convention, the proposed Convention on Human Rights and the like are undoubtedly ill-considered proposals, but the Senate itself has the power, has it but the intestinal fortitude to use it, to administer the *congé* to all such utopian projects. Can it be that some Senators prefer to be able to invoke the Constitution as a reason for doing the sensible thing rather than face up to certain pressure groups? The Bricker proposal is really a vote of lack of confidence in the political courage and integrity of the body from which it emanates.[43]

Section 3

Pro. Section 3 addressed directly the question of executive agreements. The proponents of the Bricker amendment frequently expressed a concern over the enlargement of the president's power to enter into agreements of this kind. Far more treaties than executive agreements were negotiated during the first hundred years of American history, but during the 1940s the ratio of executive agreements to treaties had become more than ten to one[44]—despite the fact that the executive agreement (as Bricker customarily pointed out) was nowhere provided for in the Constitution. As one of the Senator's allies emphasized before the Judiciary subcommittee, such agreements remained subject to the same criticism expressed in 1922 by Dr. Charles Hyde, who served as Solicitor for undersecretary of state Charles Evans Hughes: "It may be fairly doubted whether the present practice whereby the President agrees without the approval of the Senate, to understandings or declarations of vast import, serving both to further the political aspirations of other States or to weaken proportionally the subsequent influence of the United States as a deterrent, is to be regarded as advantageous to the Nation."[45]

The Bricker Revolt

Constitutional lawyers in the United States disagreed on the proper scope of executive agreements; therefore, argued the Brickerites, it would be ludicrous to presume that other nations were aware of any such limitations. "If this amendment is adopted," stated an ABA attorney, "it would put other nations on notice as to the President's power over executive agreements as they have now notice as to the limitations on his power in the treaty-making field."[46]

Lastly, the Bricker advocates cast another stone at the *Pink* case, in which the Hull-Litvinov executive agreement was held to supercede the law of the State of New York: ". . . the *Pink* case is a precedent by which any President, merely by making an executive agreement with the head of any other government, could invade vital State functions and prerogatives. It is extremely doubtful if anything would have shocked the Founding Fathers more than the suggestion that the Federal-State relationship was alterable at the will of a single individual."[47]

Con. Those opposed to the Bricker Amendment generally conceded that the principle of "judicial abstention" in the presence of "political questions" was, in Corwin's words, "pushed to an unallowable extreme" in the *Pink* case,[48] and that Yalta and Potsdam remained issues of partisan debate;[49] but the remedy to neither was to be found, they maintained, in a Constitutional amendment. Secretary of State Dulles pointed out that "[t]he danger to the nation, however, from agreements not submitted to the Senate as treaties or to the Congress for legislative validation cannot be great because, without either Senate or Congressional action, these agreements cannot constitutionally become 'law of the land.' "[50] Additionally, Congress could at any time modify an executive agreement or even repeal it—just as Congress could modify or repeal a treaty.

Moreover, the opponents stressed, Yalta and Potsdam were hardly the only examples of executive agreements. They pointed more happily to arrangements like the Rush-Bagot understanding (1817), which curbed a potential arms race between the British and the United States in the Great Lakes. Practically all questions of international aviation and international radio wavelengths, they noted, were handled by executive agreements. Commager observed at the time that, in a decade, the United States had entered into hundreds of executive agreements in the western hemisphere alone, for health and sanitation assistance, educational and cultural programs, military missions, and the shipment of military aid. His point was this: "[i]f Congress were really to pass on all these and similar agreements, it would have little time for anything else."[51] Besides, the process would create a bottleneck destroying the efficient operation of our government in its relations with foreign nations. Attorney General Brownell put it this way during the hearings:

The important fact is that under the broad grants of power in the Constitution to the Congress and to the President other procedures than formal treaty-making have developed and have been utilized throughout our history for entering into international agreements on important subject matters with more or less the same legal and practical consequences. Care must therefore be exercised, in any consideration of altering the full foreign affairs power, not to cut off, inadvertently or otherwise, functions, practices, and methods of operation that have developed usefully and to our advantage, and without which our facility in dealing with other nations would be hampered and restricted.[52]

The strongest argument advanced by the opposition, then, was that the cure would be worse than the disease. In their opinion, no text could be devised that would not restrict the president's power to negotiate treaties and safeguard the national security. The Bricker proposal would tie the president's hands and strip him of his historic control over foreign policy. The essential meaning of Section 3, said Secretary Dulles, was that "[o]ur nation's ability to deal with other nations would be gravely impaired."[53]

The Bricker Revolt

High Noon in the Senate

In his memoirs, an Eisenhower aide refers to the "showdown with Bricker" as "the greatest debate about the Constitutional ordering of our foreign relations since 1788."[54] Certainly President Eisenhower, by the summer of 1953, had begun to take the Bricker movement more seriously. Having failed to take a position against the amendment in the 1952 presidential election, he now threw his support behind a substitute amendment introduced on July 22, 1953, by Senator William F. Knowland of California, the Republican majority leader. Indeed, as Garrett reports, this proposal "was introduced largely at the behest of the Eisenhower Administration, which believed it might draw some support away from the more radical Bricker Amendment. . . ."[55] At the time, the President issued this statement: "While I have opposed other amendments which would have had the effect of depriving the President of the capacity necessary to carry on negotiations with foreign governments, I am glad to support the Knowland amendment for it confirms that this Presidential power cannot be used contrary to the Constitution. . . . Today, probably as never before in our history, it is essential that our country be able effectively to enter into agreements with other nations.

As President I have taken an oath to defend the Constitution. I therefore oppose any change which will impair the President's traditional authority to conduct foreign affairs. . . ."[56]

The first section of the Knowland Amendment simply proposed that the judicial power of the United States extend to all cases in which a conflict between a treaty and the Constitution occurred—really nothing more than a restatement of the existing provision in Article III, Section 2 of the Constitution. The second section provided for a record vote on senatorial consent to a treaty, which—though entirely sound—hardly called for a constitutional amendment; the Senate already possessed the authority to change its own rules. Finally, the third section again merely granted what the Senate already possessed: full power to concur subject to reservations when passing on treaties.[57]

In short, the Knowland Amendment was an ingenious and relatively harmless attempt at compromise. It suited the purposes of the administration by eliminating the controversial "which clause" of the Bricker Amendment, as well as any authority for Congress to "regulate" executive agreements. Senator Bricker and most of his backers immediately rejected this substitute as far too limited.[58] Some Bricker opponents also opposed the Knowland substitute on the ground that its main provisions only restated existing law, since unconstitutional treaties already have no force. They argued that no amendment of any kind was necessary.[59] Pressures for adjournment postponed further consideration of either proposal.

With the opening of the second session of the 83rd Congress in 1954, debate on S. J. Res. 1 started in earnest.[60] The drama had actually begun before the curtain went up on Capitol Hill. Between legislative sessions, Senator Bricker and his allies carried their case to the people (or, at any rate, to key conservative interest groups throughout the nation). The ranks of the pro-Brickerites swelled. The Vigilant Women for the Bricker Amendment (a "volunteer organization of housewives and mothers of boys overseas") alone presented petitions to the Senate bearing an estimated 500,000 signatures. Nor had the administration been standing by idly; its rank were now substantial, too, with the addition of the American Bar Association's Section on International and Comparative Law, the Association of the Bar of the City of New York, the American Association for the United Nations, and several liberal organizations.[61]

Despite this support for his administration, President Eisenhower now realized that his powers of agreement-making were close to being shackled. Within hours of his State of the Union

The Bricker Revolt

address, he summoned Majority Leader Knowland to the White House for a strategy session. The goal was to find some middle ground between the Knowland Amendment and the dreaded Bricker Amendment.[62] The hard fact confronting the President as he gathered with advisers was that Bricker's successful nationwide lobbying had placed the Senator in a strong bargaining position. He seemed to have garnered enough votes to push his amendment through the Congress, as well as sufficient support across the land to achieve his Constitutional amendment. At the time, one reporter observed that "the Bricker Amendment has turned into a time-bomb threat to both G.O.P. unity and White House–Congressional relations."[63] The chief difficulty was that the principal point of the Bricker Amendment (the "which clause") could not be compromised. If Senator Bricker agreed to drop this clause, he would not have compromised; he would have surrendered. Conversely, if the administration accepted the clause, it would have surrendered.[64]

On January 28, 1954, Senator Knowland placed in the *Congressional Record* an open letter to the Senate from President Eisenhower. The message was an alloy of toughness and conciliation:

> I am unalterably opposed to the Bricker Amendment. . . . We cannot hope to achieve and maintain peace if we shackle the Federal Government so that it is no longer sovereign in foreign affairs. The President must not be deprived of his historic position as the spokesman for the nation in its relations with other countries. . . . Adoption of the Bricker Amendment in its present form by the Senate would be notice to our friends as well as our enemies abroad that our country intends to withdraw from its leadership in world affairs. . . . I am aware of the feeling of many of our citizens that a treaty may override the Constitution. So that there can be no question on this point, I will gladly support an appropriate amendment that will make this clear for all time.[65]

For his part, Senator Bricker complained on the floor of the Senate that "It would be highly improper for the President of the United States to employ extralegal pressures in an effort to defeat the amendment. . . ."[66] Thus, Senator Bricker was having no part of the compromise proposal. Nor were the Democrats; at the moment, observed *Time*, "they were too busy enjoying the fun."[67]

Less than a month later, on February 26, 1954, the Bricker Amendment would be faced squarely in a final roll-call vote. Beforehand, however, the Senate witnessed a long parade of "perfecting amendments" and substitutes, accompanied by obscure parliamentary rulings. For journalist Walter Lippmann, the proposals were "one and all . . . unwashed, unpeeled, uncooked, and not yet fit to be eaten."[68] Worn down and baffled by the legal intricacies of the debate, legislators were obviously having trouble interpreting the various proposals placed before them. "None—not one of these proposals—has had the benefit of careful scrutiny," said Senator Wiley, complaining about the widespread "confusion" regarding various amendments before the chamber.[69]

The fatigue of extended debate, the constant, swirling currents of complex Supreme Court decisions (*Missouri v. Holland*, *Pink*, and the rest), along with the steady stream of arcane substitutes and amendments, had left many senators dizzy. In an effort to find solid footing, some sought refuge in more familiar terrain: the farmyard.

Senator George led the way. To illustrate his contention that executive agreements should become effective as internal law only when approved by act of Congress, the Senator declared: "I do not want a President of the U.S. to conclude an executive agreement which will make it unlawful for me to kill a cat in the back alley of my lot at night, and I do not want the President of the U.S. to make a treaty with India which would preclude me from butchering a cow in my own pasture."[70]

Senator Guy Gillette (D, Iowa) told of asking the Depart-

The Bricker Revolt

ment of State for help in distinguishing a treaty, which must be approved by the Senate, from an executive agreement, which does not. The Department of State advised that a treaty could be defined as the kind of agreement which had to be submitted to the Senate for approval. Senator Gillette said that it ". . . reminded me of the time when I was a boy on the farm and asked the hired man how to tell the difference between a male and female pigeon. He said, 'you put the corn in front of the pigeon. If he picks it up, it is a he; if she picks it up, it is a she.' "[71] Obviously, the time had come to wind up this long debate.

Despite the confusion, among the many legislative initiatives three were preeminent. First, of course, was S.J. Res. 1, the actual Bricker amendment around which the debate buzzed. Then came the Knowland Amendment (actually a series of perfecting amendments to S.J. Res. 1 advanced chiefly by Knowland and Homer Ferguson, R, Michigan).[72] Lastly came a Bricker-like amendment from the redoubtable Walter George (D, Georgia), ranking Democrat on the Foreign Relations Committee and recognized patriarch of the Senate.[73] The George Amendment was in the form of a substitute for that version of S.J. Res. 1 now heavily laden with changes added by Knowland and his allies (and by Bricker himself).

Attention focused initially on the Knowland-Ferguson amendments since, procedurally, perfecting amendments to the original S.J. Res. 1 took precedent over George's proposed substitute. At heart, these leadership amendments were designed to weaken the "which clause" of S.J. Res. 1. Following prolonged debate, the Knowland and Ferguson changes were approved, weakening the original intent of S.J. Res. 1.[74] Bricker also witnessed a steady erosion of support for what was once considered *his* amendment. Early Bricker converts, such as the highly regarded Leverett Saltonstall (R, Massachusetts), were now in retreat as the full implications of the "which clause" (and the heavy lobbying of the administration) took effect. The Bricker Amendment "went too far," Saltonstall now deduced.[75]

In a last-ditch effort to restore a winning coalition behind him, Bricker struck the "which clause" from S.J. Res. 1 with his own perfecting amendment of the George substitute and hoped for the return to the fold of Saltonstall and other backsliders. He waited in vain. On February 25, his conciliatory amendment lay dead on the Senate floor: yeas 42, nays 50.[76] John Bricker had lost control of S.J. Res. 1 to the Senate leadership forces—and his role as leader in this cause.

The Brickerites, momentarily shaken by defeat, now rallied behind their new (and more formidable) champion of states' rights, Senator George. His substitute amendment was milder than the original S.J. Res. 1, since the "which clause" was abandoned, but stronger than the leadership-diluted S.J. Res. 1. In lieu of implementing legislation by state legislatures—a sticky wicket indeed—the George Amendment settled for the less sweeping requirement of congressional implementation of executive agreements before they could have the force of domestic law. Its key sections read:

Section 1. A provision of a treaty or other international agreement which conflicts with this Constitution shall not be of any force or effect.
Section 2. An international agreement other than a treaty shall become effective as internal law in the United States only by an act of Congress.[77]

Begrudgingly, the Brickerites accepted this language as their last hope for success. As Garrett notes, the George Amendment drew "great appeal from the fact that it avoided the radicalism of the Bricker proposal while at the same time it satisfied the desire of many senators for greater control over the drawing up of executive agreements."[78]

Despite its softer language, however, the Eisenhower administration still feared the possible limitations on presidential

The Bricker Revolt

power posed by the George Amendment. The President and his aides redoubled their efforts to thwart this last charge of the Brickerites. Perhaps their most articulate ally within the Congress in defense of a strong presidency was Senator Fulbright. "It was never intended by the Founding Fathers," he said during floor debate, "that the President of the United States should be a ventriloquist's dummy sitting on the lap of the Congress."[79]

It was high noon. After some twenty days of hearings, almost 3,000 pages of printed testimony, and seemingly endless remarks on the Senate floor, the moment for the crucial votes had arrived. First would come a tally on whether the Senate chose to accept the George substitute, up or down, as the key vote on this issue (instead of the amended S.J. Res. 1). On February 26, the substitute was accepted: yeas 61, nays 30.[80] S.J. Res. 1 was now the George Amendment, and the fate of the Bricker revolt would be decided on the basis of its language. If this voting pattern held, the Brickerites would be victorious, since two-thirds of those present and voting (or 61 yeas) were required for the passage of a Constitutional amendment proposal in the Senate. Senate allies of the Eisenhower administration went into a final flurry of lobbying: at least one defector in the Bricker camp had to be found.

At last came the moment the Brickerites had worked toward for three years. "[T]he last moments of the debate," according to the *New York Times*, "were both bitter and emotional."[81] It was no doubt one of the most dramatic scenes witnessed in the Senate chamber in a decade.[82] The clerk began the slow call of the roll. Thirty minutes later, the vote was yeas 60, nays 31.[83] The George Amendment—and the Bricker movement—had failed by a solitary vote.

In the musical chairs that took place on the Senate floor between the procedural acceptance of the George Amendment for a final vote and the actual final vote, four senators "defected" from the Bricker camp and three (including Senator Knowland) from the Eisenhower camp.

Over to Bricker	Over to Eisenhower
Robert C. Hendrickson (R, New Jersey)	Ralph E. Flanders (R, Vermont)
William F. Knowland (R, California)	Lester Hill (D, Alabama)
Eugene D. Millikin (R, Colorado)	Henry M. Jackson (D, Washington)
	Warren G. Magnuson (D, Washington)

Thanks especially to the state of Washington, the President had gotten the better of the swap.

In explaining his switchover, Senator Knowland said he increasingly feared that ". . .a dangerous tendency has been developed of encroachment by the executive branch of the Government upon the proper constitutional legislative powers of the Congress."[84] It was a classic statement of the frustration felt by the Brickerites all along, words that would be repeated almost exactly by liberal senators two decades later in the shadow of the Vietnam War.

Although Senator Bricker remained defiant ("[T]he fight for protection against treaty law has only just begun"),[85] the defeat of the George Amendment marked the demise of the first congressional revolt of the postwar period. Despite subsequent Bricker-type amendments in succeeding years, none got very far in the Congress.[86] Moreover, their principal patron, John Bricker, was defeated for reelection in November 1958—ironically, on an issue involving states' rights.[87]

An Appraisal

Senator Bricker often stated that his proposal was nonpartisan; it simply represented an "honest difference of opinion in

The Bricker Revolt

the Republican Party."[88] More exactly, the proposal inflamed smoldering disagreements within both parties. The warring factions consisted of, on the one hand, those in the "internationalist" wing of their parties and, on the other hand, those more isolationist in their orientations (at least when it came to military and political pacts abroad, if not trade agreements). The first group favored ties overseas, leadership by a strong executive in foreign affairs, and participation in international organizations. The second group recoiled from all but bare-boned commitments abroad, opposed too strong an executive, and viewed the United Nations and other experiments in "world government" as anathemas.

"Spurred by the success of the Twenty-Second Amendment, the foes of Presidential power launched the Bricker amendment. . . ." writes Louis W. Koenig.[89] Beyond their fear of "presidential autocracy," the Brickerites were worried even more about the consequences of the "New Internationalism." During a hearing on the Bricker amendment, Senator Pat McCarran (D, Nevada), Chairman of the Judiciary Committee, burst out: ". . . I voted for what I consider now to be a bad treaty that I will regret probably all the days of my life . . . the United Nations."[90] For the Brickerites, international agreements had become, as one witness put it during hearings, "a kind of 'Frankenstein' instrumentality, which can change and even destroy the liberties of the American people and their form of government."[91]

Could an international agreement abrogate a statute, or affect state law beyond the enumerated powers of the Constitution? With the failure of the Bricker amendment, such questions would remain unanswered—at least by constitutional amendment. Perhaps this was for the best. As Secretary Dulles stated during hearings on the Bricker proposal, "This is an area to be dealt with by friendly cooperation between the three departments of government which are involved, rather than by

The Democratic Control of International Agreements

attempts at constitutional definition, which are futile, or by the absorption, by one branch of government, of responsibilities which are presently and properly shared."[92]

The weak spot in the Dulles prescription was the phrase "properly shared." In the decade following the Bricker amendments, a new congressional challenge would confront the making of international agreements. This time the insurgents would be internationalists in the Congress, who had come to believe that the executive branch had failed to share properly with the legislature responsibilities for American commitments abroad. They differed dramatically in ideology from their Brickerite counterparts in the fifties (see table 20 in chapter 5). This later congressional revolt is the subject of the next chapter.

Notes

1. This characterization is from "Why a Loyal Republican Wants to Limit Ike's Power," *U.S. News and World Report* 36 (January 29, 1954), p. 74; and "Knights and Knaves in Eisenhower's Great Crusade," *New Republic* 127 (July 28, 1952), p. 14.

2. 252 U.S. at 433. For a description of this case, see Arthur E. Sutherland, Jr., "Restricting the Treaty Power," *Harvard Law Review*, 65 (June 1952), pp. 1317–1318.

3. 252 U.S. at 434.

4. 315 U.S. at 230. Also see 315 U.S. at 222, where Justice Douglas says that "[w]ith one qualification, to be noted, the *Belmont* case is determinative of the present controversy." (301 U.S. 324; this case first gave legitimacy to the Litvinov Agreement.) Sutherland, op. cit., pp. 1322–1323, has a succinct description of the *Pink* case.

5. See Sutherland, "Restricting the Treaty Power," pp. 1316–1317 (note 41), and Stephen A. Garrett, "Foreign Policy and the American Constitution: The Bricker Amendment in Contemporary Perspective," *International Studies Quarterly* 16 (June 1972), p. 201 and note 6, for a description of this case and the decision. Glendon A. Schubert points out that the *Fujii* case was recognized as serving as a "catalyst" for the Bricker movement. See his "Politics and the Constitution: The Bricker Amendment during 1953," *Journal of Politics* 16 (May 1954), p. 290 (note 129).

6. *Congressional Record*, 82d Cong., 2d Sess., p. 911.

7. Interview, Professor Francis M. Carney, University of California, Riv-

The Bricker Revolt

erside, California, May 21, 1968. See also, Garrett, op. cit., p. 201. On the key Bricker Amendment, all but three of the 22 Southern senators would support Bricker.

8. Dean Acheson, *Present at the Creation: My Years in the State Department* (New York: Norton, 1969), p. 71.

9. Arthur H. Vandenberg, Jr., ed., *The Private Papers of Senator Vandenberg* (Boston: Houghton Mifflin, 1952), pp. 67–68, cited in Acheson, op. cit., pp. 71–72.

10. Acheson, *Present at the Creation*, p. 72.

11. Quoted in Henry Steele Commager, "The Perilous Folly of Senator Bricker," *The Reporter* 9 (October 13, 1953), p. 16.

12. *Cong. Rec.*, 82d Cong., 1st Sess., September 14, 1951, p. 11344. For texts of the key Bricker proposals, see Amy M. Gilbert, *Executive Agreements and Treaties, 1946–73* (Endicott, New York: Thomas-Newell, 1973), appendix 14, pp. 193–97.

13. *Cong. Rec.*, 82d Cong., 2d Sess., February 7, 1952, p. 899.

14. "Treaties and Executive Agreements," *Hearings*, Before a Subcommittee of the Committee on the Judiciary, U.S. Senate, 82d Cong., 2d Sess., May 21, 22, 27, 28, and June 9, 1952; hereafter *Hearings*, with the appropriate Congress and session.

15. Ibid., p. 21.

16. *Cong. Rec.*, 83d Cong., 1st Sess., January 7, 1953, p. 156.

17. *Hearings*, 83d Cong., 1st Sess.

18. The quote is from Amy M. Gilbert, *Executive Agreements and Treaties, 1946–1973* (Endicott, New York: Thomas-Newell, 1973), p. 65. On Eisenhower's lack of forcefulness against the Bricker initiative, see Douglas Cater, "Congress and the President," *The Reporter* 8 (May 12, 1953), pp. 15–16. In his memoirs, Eisenhower wrote that the Bricker Amendment would have spelled "chaos in international affairs." Dwight D. Eisenhower, *The White House Years: Mandate for Change, 1953–1956* (New York: Doubleday, 1963), p. 21.

19. See Garrett, "Foreign Policy and the American Constitution," pp. 197–198. For a more complete listing of the interest groups that supported Bricker, see *Hearings*, 83d Cong., 1st Sess., pp. 149–150; Schubert, op. cit., p. 287; and Gilbert, *Executive Agreements*, pp. 65–67 (note 15).

20. See *Constitutional Amendment Relative to Treaties and Executive Agreements*, Senate Report No. 412, 83d Cong., 1st Sess., June 15, 1983, p. 34.

21. *Hearings*, 82d Cong., 2d Sess., op. cit.; *Hearings*, 83d Cong., 1st Sess. op. cit.; and *Hearings*, 84th Cong., 1st Sess., April 27, 28, 29, May 2, 5, 10, 11 and 12, 1955.

22. Senate Report No. 412, op. cit.

23. *Cong. Rec.*, 83d Cong., 1st and 2d Sess.

The Democratic Control of International Agreements

24. For other discussions on the meaning of the various Bricker proposals, see *Cong. Rec.*, 83d Cong., 2d Sess., February 7, 1952, pp. 910–912; John Foster Dulles's analysis in *Hearings*, 83d Cong., 1st Sess., pp. 826–827; Marshall M. Knappen, *An Introduction to American Foreign Policy* (New York: Harper and Row, 1956), pp. 137–142; Garrett, op. cit., pp. 190–195; and Schubert, op. cit., pp. 287–297.

25. Mrs. Robert Murray, testifying in *Hearings*, 84th Cong., 1st Sess., pp. 425–426.

26. *Hearings*, 83d Cong., 1st Sess., p. 172.

27. See Garrett, "Foreign Policy and the American Constitution," p. 192.

28. *Hearings*, 83d Cong., 1st Sess., p. 905.

29. Commager, "The Perilous Folly of Senator Bricker," p. 14.

30. Edward S. Corwin, "The President's Treaty-Making Power," *Think* 19 (July 1953), p. 6. This article is reprinted in the *Cong. Rec. Appendix*, July 2, 1953 to August 28, 1953, pp. A4933–34.

31. *Cong. Rec.*, 83d. Cong., 1st Sess., March 13, 1953, p. 1952.

32. Knappen, *Introduction to American Foreign Policy*, p. 140.

33. *Hearings*, 83d Cong., 1st Sess., p. 54. His comments are on the ABA treaty proposal, but they reflect the sentiments of the Brickerites on S.J. Res. 1.

34. Ibid., p. 62.

35. See the statement by Secretary of State Dulles in ibid., p. 832.

36. See Senate Report No. 412, especially at pp. 42–44 for these arguments.

37. *Hearings*, 83d Cong., 1st Sess., p. 921.

38. Statement by the Department of State on S.J. 1 and S.J. 43, reprinted in ibid., p. 836.

39. See Commager, "The Perilous Folly of Senator Bricker," pp. 15–16, for a list of specific examples.

40. Senate Report No. 412, op. cit., p. 45.

41. According to Secretary Dulles, *Hearings*, 83d Cong., 1st Sess., p. 827.

42. See the statement by Elbert P. Tuttle, General Counsel of the Treasury, in ibid., pp. 1012–1013.

43. Corwin, "The President's Treaty-Making Power," p. 6.

44. See the table of treaties and executive agreements in Marjorie Browne, *Executive Agreements and the Congress*, Issue Brief Number IB 75035, Congressional Research Service, Washington, D.C., February 27, 1981, p. 2. Also see the table in Louis Fisher, *President and Congress* (New York: Free Press, 1972), p. 45. Obviously the executive agreements in these calculations include the statutory agreement classification introduced earlier in this study. See also Commager, op. cit., p. 16.

45. Quoted in *Hearings*, 83d Cong., 1st Sess., at p. 1171, during the testimony of George Finch, Committee on Peace and Law, American Bar Association.

46. Ibid., p. 1172.
47. Senate Report No. 412, op. cit., p. 31.
48. Corwin, "The President's Treaty-Making Power," p. 7.
49. Eisenhower's legal advisers weakly referred to Yalta and Potsdam as "political agreements" and not treaties or executive agreements. See Robert J. Donovan, *Eisenhower: The Inside Story* (New York: Harper, 1956), p. 239.
50. John Foster Dulles, "The Making of Treaties and Executive Agreements," *The Department of State Bulletin* 28 (April 20, 1953), p. 594. Dulles's views on this debate had changed dramatically since he joined the Eisenhower administration. Less than a year before being appointed Secretary of State, he told an audience of lawyers, in Louisville, Kentucky: "The treaty-making power is an extraordinary power liable to abuse. Treaties make international law and also they make domestic law. Under our Constitution treaties become the supreme law of the land. They are indeed more supreme than ordinary laws, for congressional laws are invalid if they do not conform to the Constitution, whereas treaty laws can override the Constitution. Treaties, for example, can take powers away from the State and give them to the Federal Government or to some international body and they can cut across the rights given the people by the constitutional Bill of Rights." (Cited in *Hearings*, 83d Cong., 1st Sess., p. 862.) Bricker supporters were well aware of Dulles's speech and used it frequently as ammunition in testimony before the Senate.
51. Commager, op. cit., p. 17. Also see Sutherland, op. cit., pp. 1327–1328.
52. *Hearings*, 83d Cong., 1st Sess., p. 931. Scholar John Bassett Moore reached a similar conclusion at the turn of the century. See the *Political Science Quarterly*, 20 (September 1905), p. 385.
53. "The Making of Treaties and Executive Agreements," op..cit., p. 593.
54. Donovan, op. cit., p. 231.
55. Garrett, "Foreign Policy and the American Constitution," op. cit., p. 195.
56. Reprinted in the *Cong. Rec.*, 83d Cong., 1st Sess., p. 9449. Also see William S. White, "Eisenhower Fights Bricker Pact Curb," *New York Times*, July 23, 1953.
57. See the comments by Senator Wiley in *Cong. Rec.*, 83d Cong., 1st Sess., July 22, 1953, p. 9450.
58. *Cong. Rec.*, 83d Cong., 1st Sess., August 1, 1953, pp. 10822–10829, esp. at p. 10825.
59. See, for example, Senator Wiley's comments on the Knowland Amendment in *Cong. Rec.*, 83d Cong., 1st Sess., July 22, 1953, pp. 9449–9450, and July 23, 1953, pp. 9620–9621.
60. The formal debate began on January 22, 1954. See *Cong. Rec.*, 83d Cong., 2d Sess., p. 633.
61. Donovan, *Eisenhower: The Inside Story*, p. 239.

62. "The Congress: On Their Knees," *Time* 63 (January 18, 1954), p. 20.
63. Ibid., p. 20.
64. See Commager, op. cit., p. 16.
65. *Cong. Rec.*, 83d Cong., 2d Sess., January 28, 1954, p. 933.
66. *Time* 63 (February 1, 1954), p. 11. President Eisenhower saw things differently: "As President, I had no prescribed function in the process of amending the Constitution. But as the head of government, a government that in important aspects would be seriously handicapped if this amendment were adopted, and as the head of a political party, it was my duty, in a matter of such moment to the nation's future, to participate according to my own convictions and conscience." Dwight D. Eisenhower, *The White House Years*, p. 281.
67. *Time* 63 (February 1, 1954). Neither Republican leaders in Congress nor the White House had any taste for a showdown fight on the Bricker Amendment. The reason was obvious: the resulting full-dress debate over a fundamental Constitutional issue could split the Republican Party down the middle, generate intraparty bitterness in an election year, and benefit nobody except the Democratic opposition.
68. "Today and Tomorrow," *Washington Post*, February 4, 1954. Cited in the *Cong. Rec.*, 83d Cong., 2d Sess., p. 1325.
69. *Cong. Rec.*, 83d Cong., 2d Sess., 1490.
70. Ibid., p. 1617.
71. Ibid., p. 1743.
72. This process began on February 2, 1953. See *Cong. Rec.*, 83d Cong., 2d Sess., February 2, 1954, pp. 1119–1120.
73. Ibid., January 27, 1954, p. 852.
74. *Congress and the Nation 1945–1964* (Washington, D.C.: Congressional Quarterly Service, 1965), p. 112.
75. Garrett, "Foreign Policy and the Constitution," p. 197.
76. *Cong. Rec.*, 83d Cong., 2d Sess., February 25, 1954, 2262.
77. *Cong. Rec.*, 83d Cong., 2d Sess., February 2, 1954, p. 1103.
78. Garrett, "Foreign Policy and the American Constitution," pp. 198–199.
79. *Cong. Rec.*, 83d Cong., 2d Sess., p. 1106. Use of the war-making powers by President Johnson eleven years later would dramatically change the Senator's pro-presidency stance (see chapter 5).
80. *Cong. Rec.*, 83d Cong., 2d Sess., February 26, 1974, p. 2358.
81. William S. White, "Senate Defeats All Plans to Check Treaty Powers; Final Vote Margin is One Vote," *New York Times*, February 27, 1954.
82. Ibid.
83. *Cong. Rec.*, 83d Cong., 2d Sess., February 26, 1954, p. 2374.
84. White, "Senate Defeats All Plans," p. 2332.
85. *Cong. Rec.*, 83d Cong., 2d Sess., August 5, 1954, p. 13457.
86. Senator Bricker continued to introduce similar constitutional amendment resolutions in 1954, in 1955, and in 1957.

The Bricker Revolt

87. See James A. Maxwell, "The Battle Bricker Didn't Want to Fight," *The Reporter* 19 (November 27, 1958), p. 19. The issue was a right-to-work amendment. With Bricker removed from the scene, the leading flag-bearers for this cause became the colorful Minority Leader Everett McKinley Dirksen (R, Illinois) and Louisiana Democrats Allen J. Ellender and Russell B. Long.

88. *Newsweek* 65 (January 10, 1955), p. 20.

89. Louis W. Koenig, *The Chief Executive* (New York: Harcourt, Brace, and World, 1964), p. 7. The Twenty-Second Amendment, ratified in 1951, limited the tenure of presidents to two terms.

90. *Hearings*, Committee on the Judiciary, U.S. Senate, 82d Cong., 1st Sess., p. 145.

91. Frank Holman testifying in *Hearings*, 85th Cong., 1st Sess., p. 423.

92. *Hearings*, 83d Cong., 1st Sess., p. 828.

5.

A Second Resurgence

> Even the wisest and most competent of presidents is still a human being, susceptible to human flaws and human failures of judgment. The greatest insight of our Founding Fathers was their recognition of the dangers of unlimited power exercised by a single man or institution; their greatest achievement was the safeguards against absolute power which they wrote into our Constitution.
>
> —FRANK CHURCH, *Congressional Record*, APRIL 30, 1970

Restoring a Constitutional Balance

The underlying objective of the Bricker amendment, observed Senator Fulbright in 1954, was "a retreat from the world."[1] A second uprising in Congress against presidential discretion over commitments abroad, led by Fulbright and others, also exhibited ironically a jaded outlook on unwarranted involvement around the globe. "Come home, America!" said one of its spokesmen, Senator George McGovern (D, South Dakota), in a 1972 presidential campaign speech. Beware the "apostles of interventionism," warned Senator Church in one of his 1976 presidential campaign speeches. Critics dubbed these new legislative insurgents the "neo-isolationists."[2]

A Second Resurgence

The appellation was misleading, however. The Brickerites and the insurgents of the next generation were worlds apart in philosophy and tactics. The Brickerites opposed continued United States participation in the UN, eyed skeptically American involvement in other multinational organizations ("backdoor approaches to world government," admonished a leading Bricker Amendment lobbyist),[3] worried chiefly about undue executive discretion to change *domestic* law through international agreements, and sought sweeping constitutional changes in the conduct of foreign agreement-making.

In contrast, the neo-insurgents accepted the UN as a modestly useful forum, extolled the virtues of some other multinational entities (notably NATO, the International Court of Justice, and various collective-security arrangements to protect core interests), worried chiefly about undue executive discretion to change *foreign* policy through the unwise involvement of United States military personnel in regions of *peripheral* interest, and pursued comparatively modest reforms to limit executive discretion.

If the Brickerites were in full retreat from the world (something of an exaggeration—even Bricker valued NATO), the neo-insurgents were in partial retreat. They opposed an over-extension of American commitments to far-flung corners of the globe that appeared of dubious relevance to the well-being of the United States. Not even George McGovern wanted America to come home from everywhere, just from Third World backwaters where we had no business. "Our gravest mistakes in the last twenty years have come from the assumption that we have the wealth and power to mold the world to our own liking," said Senator Church in 1970, with reference to the underdeveloped countries. "We don't, and the sooner we learn to impose some reasonable restraint on our own tendency to intervene too much in other people's affairs, the happier land we will have and the less burden we will place upon our own people to undertake sacrifices that are not really related to their own good or the good of the country."[4]

What Fulbright, McGovern, Church, and their allies lamented most was American entry into the swampland of Vietnam, with its great toll of blood and treasure. As conservatives out of the Bricker mold rallied behind the Vietnam War as a vital test of America's will to resist global communism, liberals and moderates—often sounding like Brickerites—fought to limit the power of the president to continue or expand the war. The tables were turned. In the fifities, the rallying cry of the Brickerites was "Protect States' Rights!" Now, for the neo-insurgents, the cry was "No More Vietnams!"

Despite fundamental disagreements on policy objectives, the Brickerites and the Vietnam insurgents were closely wedded in their belief in one bedrock principle: a distrust of executive discretion in foreign policy. Resist executive "encroachment," argued Senator Knowland in 1954; "Swing back the pendulum," urged Senator Church in 1970.[5] Ultimately, what both movements desired was not foreign policy by the executive or by the Congress, but a "constitutional balance" between the two (to use a favorite phrase from both eras). As Stephen A. Garrett has aptly written, these movements were "substantially focused on the necessity of reasserting the prerogatives and status of the Congress as such if that institution is to maintain its vitality as a central component of the American Constitutional system."[6]

Mandatory Reporting

Efforts to restore a Constitutional balance in foreign policy during the sixties were stimulated initially by a growing resentment on Capitol Hill toward the foreign policies of President Lyndon Johnson. Senator Fulbright, then Chairman of the Foreign Relations Committee, was, until 1965, an arch-defender of presidential prerogatives in foreign affairs, but the President's misrepresentations over (and eventual invasion of)

A Second Resurgence

the Dominican Republic soured his relations with Johnson. Waves of skepticism moved across the Senate from the Foreign Relations Committee epicenter.

The intensity of this new mood increased as more representatives began to question the wisdom of the war in Vietnam and the odor of executive mendacity that seemed to surround it. In August 1964, President Johnson had asked for, and received, open-ended authority to respond to military threats in Indochina (following an alleged attack by North Vietnamese boats against United States destroyers on a foggy night in the Gulf of Tonkin). The so-called Gulf of Tonkin Resolution, adopted almost unanimously on August 10 (two legislators dissented) without hearings and after only two days of debate, provided congressional approval to "take all necessary steps, including the use of armed force" in Indochina (Pub. L. 88-408). The resolution was later claimed by the Johnson administration to be the "functional equivalent" of a congressional declaration of war.[7]

By 1965, some senators had begun to regret this blank check they had given the President, and claimed they had no idea he planned to use the resolution as authority to send half a million American soldiers into a full-blown war in Indochina. They would now try to put the horse back into the barn.

First came individual pronouncements against the Vietnam War; then, sharply critical hearings in 1966 held by the Senate Foreign Relations Committee. Then, in February 1967, the Senate passed Resolution 40, which established a Senate Subcommittee on Separation of Powers.[8] Led by Sam Ervin (D, North Carolina), who would subsequently chair the Senate Watergate investigation, this Subcommittee held extensive and highly critical hearings on the use of executive agreements.

In 1968, President Johnson hastily requested the Senate to approve a broadly worded resolution on foreign aid. On the eve of a hemispheric summit meeting in Punta del Esta, the President sought congressional support for costly new agreements

The Democratic Control of International Agreements

with the nations of Latin America. Once burned twice shy, the Senate Foreign Relations Committee refused to write another blank check, and instead passed (by a vote of 9 to 0) a substitute resolution stating that new foreign aid initiatives in Latin American would be given due consideration in accordance with the Committee's normal legislative timetable.[9] With this shot, the Foreign Relations Committee went beyond words to deeds in its search for an acceptable balance between the Congress and the executive branch in foreign policy. The mood of skepticism on Capitol Hill had changed to outright defiance. An institutional revolution was underway.

In February 1969, the Senate Foreign Relations Committee created a special subcommittee to examine executive-induced commitments abroad: the Ad Hoc Subcommittee on United States Security Agreements and Commitments Abroad (the Symington Subcommittee). Its detailed findings (some of which were presented in chapter 3) laid out in greater detail than ever before the alarming extent of executive discretion to commit the country overseas—especially through secret military agreements. From these findings and the growing disenchantment with President Johnson's successor, Richard Nixon, who seemed equally bogged down in the Vietnam War, came the National Commitments Resolution (S. Res. 85) in June 1969. It stated: "Be it resolved, that it is the sense of the Senate that a national commitment by the United States to a foreign power necessarily and exclusively results from affirmative action taken by the executive and *legislative* branches of the United States Government through means of a treaty, convention, or other *legislative* instrumentality specifically intended to give effect to such a commitment" (emphasis added). Then came the Church Resolution in December 1970 regarding the Spanish bases agreement (see chapter 3). The Senate moved ever closer to pinpointing a major villain in this drama: the misused executive agreement.

A Second Resurgence

Finally, in 1972, the Senate took its longest step toward tighter control over agreement-making. So far, the Senate had just passed resolutions. Though some were toughly worded, they expressed only a point of view and were not legally binding. Now the Senate turned to statutory remedies. From a sense of despair over the failure of Congress to know what commitments the executive branch was making overseas (especially in Indochina), Senator Case introduced legislation to remove this blind spot. Widely regarded as the chief architect in the rebuilding of congressional authority in the agreement-making area, he sought to guarantee that Congress had access to information about all commitments abroad. To this end, the Case Act was passed in the Senate by a vote of 81 to 0.[10] Clement Zablocki (D, Wisconsin) introduced the same measure in the House; six months later, the Case-Zablocki Act was passed there as well by voice vote, and signed into law by President Nixon on August 22, 1972.[11]

Henceforth, the Department of State would have to report all statutory and executive agreements to Congress within sixty days. The language reads:

The Secretary of State shall transmit to the Congress the text of any international agreement, other than a treaty, to which the United States is a party as soon as practicable after such agreement has entered into force with respect to the United States but in no event later than sixty days thereafter. However, any such agreement the immediate public disclosure of which would, in the opinion of the President, be prejudicial to the national security of the United States shall not be so transmitted to the Congress but shall be transmitted to the Committee on Foreign Relations of the Senate and the Committee on Foreign Affairs of the House of Representatives under an appropriate injunction of secrecy to be removed only upon due notice from the President.[12]

While hesitant and cautious compared to the bold initiatives of the Brickerites to amend the Constitution (and compared to harsher proposals that would soon follow), the Case-Zablocki Act

The Democratic Control of International Agreements

represents nonetheless a significant move by Congress toward an institutional sharing of power in foreign affairs. As members of the Foreign Relations Committee noted in a report issued during debate on the Case proposal:

> . . . the principle of mandatory reporting of agreements with foreign countries to the Congress is more than desirable; it is, from a constitutional standpoint, crucial and indispensable. For the Congress to accept anything less would represent a resignation from responsibility and an alienation of an authority which is vested in the Congress by the Constitution. If Congress is to meet its responsibilities in the formulation of foreign policy, no information is more crucial than the fact and content of agreements with foreign nations.[13]

Besides setting a specific time limit for reporting, the Case-Zablocki Act reawakened the executive branch (and, to some extent, the public) to the continuing problems of unwarranted executive agreements. The Department of State was now forced to improve its own reporting procedures and to pay more attention to the international negotiations of agencies throughout the government. Indeed, according to a close observer, "State used [the Case-Zablocki Act] to strengthen its hand over the agencies—to centralize its authority."[14]

The Case-Zablocki Act, then, has been the most successful of the various attempts to restore congressional powers over agreement-making, no doubt because it has also been the least demanding and controversial. Despite its virtues, the imperfections of Case-Zablocki have become evident over the past decade. The sixty-day provision in the law, for example, permits the executive branch to inform the Congress *after* a commitment has already been made to another country. Presented with a fait accompli, Congress is left playing catch-up—with all the momentum on the side of the executive. While Congress now has more complete information, and sooner, than under an old and inadequate 1950 reporting statute,[15] its ability to help shape the outcome of a commitment is still severely restricted.

A Second Resurgence

With its late awareness of a sealed negotiation, Congress is faced with either going along or wrecking the arrangements by shutting off funds or otherwise barring implementation. This "take it or leave it" situation is a far cry from the constitutional partnership that motivated the Vietnam insurgents.

Exacerbating this ex post facto reporting is the lateness in arrival of the reports on Capitol Hill. Often the executive branch fails to meet the sixty-day deadline; in fact, some agreements are forwarded as much as a year late.[16] In 1977, a staff aide on the Senate Foreign Relations Committee documented that about 39 percent of the agreements reported in 1976 were beyond the sixty-day limit, with nearly 50 percent late as a result of delay by other executive agencies in reporting to the Department of State (which is supposed to serve as a clearinghouse and transmitter to Congress).[17] The next two years showed some improvement, according to a Senate Foreign Relations Committee internal memo: in 1977, the tardiness figure fell to 32 percent, and in 1978 to 25 percent—still a sizable proportion in light of the clear language in the statute setting a sixty-day limit.[18]

"The reports come up here so late, we have to rely on contacts and leaks in the executive branch to find out when really important negotiations are underway," says a frustrated Senate staff aide with foreign policy responsibilities.[19] A House staffer in a comparable position states flatly that he does not rely much on the reports forwarded by the Department of State, but also depends upon his "sources" in the executive branch to "tip me off if something controversial is in the works." Hearings on significant commitments, he adds, "are triggered almost always by this informal alarm system, not by Case-Zablocki paperwork."[20] Legislative oversight reliant upon informal (and possibly haphazard) leaks hardly seems to be in the spirit of the original law

Some of these shortcomings in the reporting system are a

product of the severe strains placed upon the Office of Treaty Affairs in the Department of State. It is understaffed and has trouble meeting its new obligations under the Case-Zablocki Act. The problem, though, obviously goes beyond the need for more analysts and clerical assistants in this office. Obviously, other agencies within the executive branch have been negligent in their response to the reporting requirements, and their responsiveness has worsened (at least during the 1976–78 period, for which data is available). In 1976, 49 percent of all agreements that arrived late to Congress had been received late by the State Department from other agencies. In 1977, the figure rose to 63 percent, and, in 1978, to 64 percent.[21]

When explaining the lateness of a report, the Department of State points to several reasons. Predominant among them are: late transmittals from other agencies; initial ambiguity over whether an agreement is significant enough to be reported under Case-Zablocki; "inadvertent delay;" and late transmittals from diplomatic posts. A closer examination of the reporting pattern for 1978 (see table 18) illustrates the frequency of these explanations.

Over the years, State has shown some improvements in correcting tardiness at its end, but growing delays at the agencies' end have offset these improvements—even though a 1977 amendment to the Case-Zablocki Act requires executive agencies engaged in agreement-making to furnish them to the Department of State within twenty days after they have been signed.[22] Despite the 1977 Amendment, as of 1979 only three agencies (the Departments of Defense, Commerce, and Health and Human Resources) had written regulations instructing their personnel to forward international agreements to the Department of State, and none required the transmittal to be accomplished within the twenty-day limit of the statute.[23] As David J. Kuchenbecker has noted, the situation was one of "widespread lack of cooperation" by the agencies in helping the Department of State fulfill the requirements of Case-Zablocki.[24]

A Second Resurgence

Table 18
International Agreements (Other Than Treaties): A Frequency Distribution of Late Submissions to the U.S. Senate Committee on Foreign Relations, 1978[a]

Total Submissions	% Agreements
504	100.0%
Late Submissions by Time	
six weeks or less	2.8
More than six weeks	19.9
More than one year	2.8
TOTAL	25.5
Late Submissions by Explanation	
Late from agencies	63.6
Initial definitional ambiguity	3.1
"Inadvertent" delay	8.5
Late from diplomatic post	6.2
Other	18.6

[a] Based on figures kept by the Senate Foreign Relations Committee, March 12, 1979.

Most alarming, of course, is when international agreements fail to be reported at all. Kuchenbecker's inquiries in January 1978 revealed that "few major agencies could indicate even the number of international agreements they had entered into during the previous year."[25] In 1975, Representative Les Aspin (D, Wisconsin) estimated that some four hundred to six hundred of the international agreements concluded since passage of the Case-Zablocki Act had not been sent to Congress, because the executive branch had redefined what needed to be reported to suit its own purposes.[26]

Intelligence agreements provide a rigorous test of executive branch reporting under the Case-Zablocki Act. Around a hundred secret agreements have been reported to Congress since the inception of the Case-Zablocki legislation,[27] but fragments of evidence suggest that some efforts have been made here to bypass the reporting requirements. For example, in 1975, the chief Department of State Legal Adviser of Treaty Affairs told a Senate judiciary subcommittee he had not yet determined whether six agreements between United States intelligence agencies and their foreign counterparts were subject to the legislative reporting requirements.[28] Moreover, according to another seasoned Department of State specialist on treaty affairs, the intelligence agencies have shifted perceptibly to oral "understandings" since the Case-Zablocki bill, in order to avoid reporting these commitments to Congress.[29] A letter from the House Committee on Intelligence, written soon after its creation in 1977, to the CIA requesting systematic reporting on major collection operations, counterintelligence missions, and covert actions was substantially ignored; only important covert actions were reported to the Committee, as required by the Hughes-Ryan Act (passed in December 1974), along with information on a few collection operations.[30]

The most compelling evidence that something was amiss surfaced as a result of a General Accounting Office (GAO) investigation. In February 1976, a GAO report stated that the transmission of executive agreements to the legislative branch suffered from significant omissions. The report, which examined only American agreements with the Republic of Korea, documented more than thirty instances since the passage of the Case-Zablocki Act when agreements had not been sent to the Congress. Several dealt with military matters, such as the joint use of Taegu Air Base and the transfer of $37.6 million worth of military equipment to Korean forces. With classic bureaucratic understatement, the GAO investigators concluded: "We feel that certain arrangements identified in our study which were not transmitted to Congress . . . would have been of interest to that body had they been so transmitted."[31] The most disturbing aspect of the GAO findings was that the Korean agreements were reported neither to the Congress nor to the Department of State.

Clearly, government agencies—including the Department of

A Second Resurgence

Defense—have negotiated and transacted international agreements on an agency-to-agency basis without sufficient monitoring by the Department of State itself, let alone by congressional overseers. One can have only sympathy for both the Department of State and the Congress; the number of American agencies involved in international agreement-making has proliferated at such a rapid rate that the task of monitoring these commitments has become staggering. As Joseph S. Nye, Jr., has noted: "Nearly all the major executive departments have little foreign offices of their own. In 1973, for example, of 19,000 Americans abroad on diplomatic missions, only 3,400 were from the State Department and less than half of the government delegates accredited to international conferences came from the State Department."[32] Similarly, Raymond Hopkins comments that, "With over 700 international conferences a year, transnational collegiums of professionals in agriculture, atomic energy, meteorology, satellites, and health tend to work directly with one another with little supervision by the foreign policy agencies (basically State) in staffing conferences, drawing up technical guidelines or reaching consensual decisions."[33]

Everyone wants in on the act, it seems, from the Interior Department to the Smithsonian Institution and the regulatory agencies.[34] This Balkanization, in Kuchenbecker's words, has introduced "a new era in treaty practice," one in which compliance by agency chiefs in the reporting of agency-to-agency agreements has been "mixed at best" and heavily dependent upon the "discretion and goodwill" of the agencies.[35]

Shaken by the GAO report on Korea, Congress and the Department of State have taken steps to try to overcome these powerful centrifugal forces. Even before the GAO inquiry, State emphasized to the other executive agencies the importance of interagency coordination of agreement reporting under Case-Zablocki. "I want to invite your personal attention," wrote Acting Secretary of State Kenneth Rush to agency heads in 1973, "to the problem of ensuring that all international agreements to which the United States becomes a party are cleared, prior to conclusion, with the Department of State. . . ."[36] A Department of State legal adviser considered this interagency memorandum tantamount to a *requirement* to report.[37]

After the GAO report, pressures from the Department of State on the other agencies increased as Congress made its displeasure plain to State. On March 9, 1976, the Department of State Legal Adviser for Treaty Affairs, Monroe Leigh, sent to all diplomatic posts an airgram clarifying Case-Zablocki procedures and emphasizing that henceforth agency-to-agency agreements should be treated with the gravity of executive agreements.[38] Agency-to-agency agreements (of the kind unearthed by the GAO inquiry) were now officially recognized as legally binding international agreements, reportable under Case-Zablocki if deemed appropriate by State. If an agency-to-agency agreement were politically significant in the opinion of State, or if it involved substantial cash flows, or substantial transnational cooperation in a policy area (say, communications), the agreement would be forwarded to Congress. A similar notice went from Leigh to agency heads three days later.[39] The result was an upsurge in agreements sent to Captiol Hill, from an annual average of 258 during the 1972 to 1975 period to 458 for 1976 through mid-1978.[40] The distribution for 1976 and 1977 by agency, according to a Library of Congress calculation, is shown in table 19.[41]

The Monroe memorandum stimulated the establishment of improved internal procedures in some agencies. A November 3, 1976, Department of Defense (DOD) "Directive on International Agreements" required the transmittal of foreign agreements to the DOD Assistant General Counsel within fifteen days. All DOD officials had to have, henceforth, prior written approval from the Assistant Secretary of Defense for International Security Affairs before negotiating an international agreement. "The experience factor is low . . ." cautioned one in-house appraisal of these new regulations.[42]

A Second Resurgence

Table 19
International Agreements Submitted to Congress by Executive Agencies, 1976 and 1977[a]

Executive Agency	Number of Agreements
Department of State	441
Agency for International Development	271
Department of Defense	45
Department of Justice	20
Nuclear Regulatory Commission	21
Department of Treasury	13
Department of Transportation	12
National Science Foundation	10
United States Postal Service	10
Special Trade Representative	8
Atomic Energy Commission	8
Department of Commerce	1
Others	45

[a] Compiled by Marjorie Ann Browne, Congressional Research Service, Library of Congress.

The issue drew President Jimmy Carter's attention in April 1977. In a memorandum to high officials in his administration, the President ordered: "All proposals beyond or in addition to approved budgets to foreign governments or international organizations should . . . be submitted to me for approval jointly through the Director, Office of Management and Budget, and the Assistant to the President for National Security Affairs before any commitment, formal or informal, is made."[43]

Despite these efforts, reporting from the agencies continued to be far from ideal (as the figures of table 18 illustrate). To tighten the screws still further, the 1977 amendment to Case-Zablocki was passed. Congress was losing patience. The law "is not being complied with," grumbled the Chairman of the Senate Foreign Relations Committee, John Sparkman (D, Alabama), and the Ranking Minority Member, Senator Case, in a letter to the Secretary of State, which arrived on the heels of the new amendment. If compliance were not immediately forthcoming, they added, the Foreign Relations Committee

The Democratic Control of International Agreements

might propose legislation to make all late agreements "without force and effect."[44] Here were fighting words; yet still, the agencies behaved sluggishly in their compliance. Apparently, Congress needed a two-by-four to get the attention of the bureaucratic mules.

The two-by-four was pulled out the next year in the form of an amendment to the State Department Authorization Act for fiscal 1979, signed into law by President Carter on October 7, 1978.[45] This second try at amending and strengthening Case-Zablocki had three primary objectives. First, it required reduction to writing and subsequent submission of "any oral international agreements." Second, it required a presidential explanation of all late agreements (that is, beyond the sixty-day limit), and, third, it enhanced State's control over agency-to-agency agreements by mandating State-agency consultation before the signing of an international agreement. (Congress, however, shied away at the last minute from requiring outright Department of State *approval* of all agreements.) As one authority aptly concluded, Congress's patience was "clearly at an end."[46]

Despite its obvious impatience, Congress did provide some latitude to the executive branch in the 1978 amendment. The Secretary of State was allowed to determine whether "an agreement constitutes an international agreement within the meaning of this section," and the president (through the efforts of the secretary of state) could "promulgate such rules and regulations as may be necessary to carry out" the changes.

These changes helped tighten Department of State control over the reporting procedure, and concentrated accountability for easier monitoring by the legislative branch. Nonetheless, the number of late agreements reported was still substantial in 1978 and 1979. According to the first report under this new law, 132 agreements were late in transmittal to Congress during 1979; the number dropped significantly the next year, yet still totaled 46 agreements.[47] Progress has been achieved toward compliance under the Case-Zablocki Act and its amendments; but

A Second Resurgence

clearly, problems persist even with the relatively simple reporting requirement.

Even though the transmittal of oral agreements "reduced to writing" is now required, this aspect of agreement-making remains a difficult one for the Congress. Since the universe of such pacts is ultimately determined by the executive branch, some slippage in reportage is likely. What will be the dispensation of "understandings" or "private exchanges" now? Such commitments can be viewed by foreign governments as solemn assurances every inch as binding as formal treaties. The experiences with President Nixon's secret message in 1973 to North Vietnam, the Sinai "understanding," and the Helsinki Accord (see chapter 3) are too fresh to be forgotten. In each instance, the executive branch tried to justify an exception from Case-Zablocki obligations on policy grounds. For the secret message, the "sensitivity" of the issue was the primary justification; for the Sinai understanding, the Department of State thought this was simply a proper exercise of executive authority, divorced from normal agreement-making provisions; for Helsinki, the accord was not really an agreement, State argued, but rather a "political statement of intent." One must wonder about possible misuse of the latitude given in the 1978 amendment to State as the final arbiter of what constitutes a reportable international agreement.

Lest the executive branch bear all the blame for shortcomings in the implementation of Case-Zablocki, note that Congress, too, has failed to respond fully to its responsibilities. The fault lies not in its written procedures, which are reasonably thorough. On the Senate Foreign Relations Committee, for example, the committee *Manual* requires these steps for handling international agreements reported under the Case-Zablocki Act:

1. Executive agreements will be routed promptly to the staff member primarily responsible for the country involved. Where an agreement

The Democratic Control of International Agreements

cuts across geographic and functional areas, both staff members concerned should be made aware of the agreement.

2. Within one week after receipt of an agreement, the staff member concerned will return it to the Deputy Chief of Staff with a very brief summary and analysis.

3. In analyzing an agreement, the staff member should satisfy himself that there is legal authority for it, that it is consistent with views expressed by the Committee or by individual Senators, and that it does not raise new questions of public policy.

4. If an agreement does not meet all these criteria, the staff member should so note in his summary and analysis and should also recommend action to be taken. When in doubt, consult with the Chief or his deputy.

5. Each week the summaries and analyses will be circulated to members of the Committee as an appendix to the *Weekly Summary*.

6. Classified agreements will be handled in the same way, except that the summary and analysis will not be included in the *Weekly Summary* but will be communicated to Senators separately under the appropriate security safeguards.[48]

On this committee, the staff has even developed a modest computer storage system within its offices, whereby all recent international agreements can be retrieved and presented on a display screen by date of signing, target country, and general subject area. Rather than wading through piles of documents, a committee staffer is now able, with a few taps on the computer keyboard, to display instantaneously, say, all United States–Saudi Arabian agreements of recent vintage. (This project has low priority on the committee and the staff has been unable to code in more than recent agreements so far. See chapter 6 for recommendations on a computer-assisted monitoring system for international agreements.)

Procedures on the House Foreign Affairs Committee are substantially more antiquated. A single staffer (compared to three or four involved at one point or another in the Senate committee) receives the reports from the Department of State and circulates a brief memorandum to committee members and key

A Second Resurgence

staff, outlining the substance of each agreement. These documents are then filed by hand according to date of receipt, with little hope of simple retrieval by country or subject matter. A recent example of a circulated memorandum is presented in figure 5.

The descriptions of the agreements are, to put it gently, succinct. The same is true for comparable memos circulated through the Senate Foreign Relations Committee. A frustrated Senate aide offers this explanation: "The sketchy background statements [prepared by the Department of State] accompanying the agreements are practically useless for someone trying to figure out the anticipated effect of the commitments."[49] This, of course, begs the question as to why the committees have failed to require more detailed reports from the executive branch.

In short, Congress has not really done much with the reports forwarded from the Department of State. "They just get filed away in drawers," complains one exasperated official in the Office of Treaty Affairs who invests considerable time in their collation.[50] While this is an exaggeration, it is true that incoming Case-Zablocki reports rarely receive the close analysis some of them warrant. The reports are too superficial to begin with and, of equal importance, the press of seemingly more urgent business is too great—confirmation hearings, foreign crises, speechwriting, tomorrow morning's hearings, constituent requests, and the like. As a candid Senator Hubert H. Humphrey (D, Minnesota) once observed, "We've been too busy to follow up—that's the problem."[51]

The weakest feature of the Case-Zablocki reporting procedure, however, continues to be the submissive acceptance by Congress of ex post facto notifications. A true institutional partnership in foreign policy can only be based on a system of prior notification, before a commitment is sealed. This is what Senator Arthur H. Vandenberg (R, Michigan) had in mind with his famous admonishment to the Truman administration that leg-

Figure 5
U.S. House of Representatives, Committee on Foreign Affairs, Memorandum on International Agreements Submitted to Congress, October 1982.

COMMITTEE ON FOREIGN AFFAIRS

October 5, 1982

MEMORANDUM

TO: MEMBERS OF THE COMMITTEE ON FOREIGN AFFAIRS

SUBJ: International Agreements Submitted to Congress

The Committee on Foreign Affairs has received *Executive Communication 4879* submitting a list of international agreements other than treaties concluded by the Executive Branch.

If, after receiving the listing, you wish to read the text of an agreement, you may do so in the Office of the Committee on Foreign Affairs, which is the official repository under Public Law 92-403.

September 29, 1982

INTERNATIONAL AGREEMENTS OTHER THAN TREATIES TRANSMITTED IN ACCORDANCE WITH PUBLIC LAW 92-403

1. Arrangement between the United States and Switzerland for the exchange of technical information and cooperation in nuclear safety matters, with patent addendum. Signed at Bethesda and Bern July 20 and August 10, 1982. Entered into force August 10, 1982.
2. Agreement between the United States and Madagascar for sales of agricultural commodities, relating to the agreement of August 19, 1981 (TIAS 10218). Signed at Antananarivo August 12, 1982. Entered into force August 12, 1982.
3. Agreement between the United States and Argentina amending the agreement of September 22, 1977, as amended, relating to air transport services (TIAS 8978; 29 UST 27795). Effected by exchange of letters at Buenos Aires August 13, 1982. Entered into force August 13, 1982.
4. Agreement between the United States and Haiti relating to the establishment of a Peace Corps program in Haiti. Effected by exchange of notes at Port-au-Prince August 12 and 13, 1982. Entered into force August 13, 1982.

MULTILATERAL

5. Memorandum of understanding concerning transatlantic scheduled service air fares, with annexes. Done at Washington May 2, 1982. Entered into force August 1, 1982.

A Second Resurgence

islators want to be in on the "take-offs," not just the "crash landings" in foreign affairs.[52]

Beyond Case-Zablocki

In some policy areas, the Congress has crept beyond the rudimentary reporting provisions of the Case-Zablocki Act toward the concept of prior notification—and even consultation. This more aggressive posture has taken four legislative forms: statutory language compelling prior notification of international agreements; stronger language permitting a congressional veto of unwarranted agreements; stronger still, language requiring a positive majority vote in Congress for approval of selected agreements (more than a passive opportunity for veto); and, strongest, the mandatory use of the formal treaty-making procedure for "significant" agreements.

Prior notice. The intelligence policy area illustrates well a slow evolution by the Congress toward a partnership (still imperfect) in foreign policy-making based on a shared access to information.[53] From 1947 (when the CIA was established) to 1974, Congress had—and sought—little information about intelligence agreements abroad. Then with passage of the Hughes-Ryan Act in December 1974, it began to receive "in a timely fashion" information on covert action (CA) agreements.

This phrase "in a timely fashion" was still post hoc (interpreted by the CIA, with one exception, to mean within twenty-four hours);[54] but it represented a great advance over the indefinite expectations of the earlier era—at least within the limited scope of covert action. Reporting requirements for intelligence collection and counterintelligence (CI) agreements remained nonexistent. In 1980, however, Congress took a step further, under the leadership of its intelligence committees, with passage of the Intelligence Accountability Act.[55]

This 1980 Intelligence Act cast out "in a timely fashion" in favor of including reports on "any significant *anticipated* intel-

The Democratic Control of International Agreements

ligence activity" (emphasis added), a phrase drawn from the old Atomic Energy Act. This spelled out a congressional intent favoring prior notification, and, it was clear, not just for covert action, but across the range of intelligence activities (to include significant CA, CI, and collection agreements reached with other nations). So the Congress now claimed the right to monitor all important intelligence operations, to have access to any other information it wished, and to have reports in advance. Here, at least on paper, was legislative oversight with real meaning; no more faits accomplis from the intelligence community.

One must emphasize *on paper*, however, for the monitoring of international agreements—like everything else Congress does—depends so much on the attitudes and personalities of the legislators involved.[56] Despite the strong sword provided by the 1980 act, the Senate Select Committee on Intelligence (once aggressive under the leadership of Daniel K. Inouye, D, Hawaii and his successor, Birch Bayh, D, Indiana) has lately chosen to return to the pre-1974 "know-nothing" era (with the exception of a few committee members, like Daniel Patrick Moynihan, D, New York, and Joseph Biden, D, Delaware, who try against heavy odds to carry out the spirit of the 1980 legislation). The chairman of the committee, Barry Goldwater, summed up his views for the *Washington Post:* "I don't even like to have an intelligence oversight committee. I don't think it's any of our business."[57]

The question of monitoring important intelligence agreements with other nations is apparently of little concern to most Senate Intelligence Committee members; indeed, the committee fails even to receive reports of secret intelligence agreements, as required by the Case-Zablocki Act.[58] Fortunately for the concept of checks and balances in the foreign policy field, the House Select Committee on Intelligence has been somewhat more robust in its scrutiny of intelligence operations and— after over a year of arm-wrestling with the intelligence com-

A Second Resurgence

munity—now receives regular reports on international agreements touching on intelligence matters[59]—though how truly comprehensive this reporting is remains open to question.

Regardless of its uneven application, the 1980 Intelligence Act stands as a benchmark in congressional efforts to enhance the participation of elected representatives in the making of international agreements. It achieves—in law—equal access to information, and makes that information available to legislators before it is too late for them to use it.[60] Without these provisions, legislative counsel in foreign policy becomes a mockery; with them, plus true consultation, the nation benefits from the ample advantages of a genuine institutional partnership.

Congressional veto. A standard definition of the congressional (or legislative) veto is "a statutory provision that delays an announced administrative action, usually for a specified number of days, during which time Congress may vote to approve or disapprove the action without further Presidential involvement."[61] As with statutes designed to solicit advance notification, the congressional veto has been used (notes a House Foreign Affairs Committee report) "as a basic device for insuring effective prior consultation by the executive branch."[62] Before the congressional veto was struck down by the Supreme Court as unconstitutional in 1983, it was used in a wide range of foreign policy areas: war powers, arms transfers, nuclear nonproliferation, international trade, and foreign aid, among others.[63] The Atomic Energy Act of 1954, the Trade Act of 1975, and the Fishery Conservation and Management Act of 1976, for instance, contained a provision giving Congress the right to disapprove within sixty days any agreement made pursuant to the legislation. Similar language was written into a law on arms sales, as a result of amendments introduced by Senator Gaylord Nelson (D, Wisconsin) and Representative Jonathan Bingham (D, New York) to the 1974 Foreign Assistance Act. Any intended sale of defense articles or services worth $25 million or more had to be reported to the Congress. In turn, the Congress could disallow any sale by a majority vote in both chambers within twenty days. By 1976, this amendment was modified to include the sale of any major defense item costing $7 million or more, and the review time was lengthened to thirty days. Since then, a procedure was worked out between the executive branch and the Congress whereby a total of fifty days of congressional review were allowed, twenty days of "informal notification" and thirty days of "formal notification." This procedure was followed in the sale of AWACS (Airborne Warning and Control System, a sophisticated radar-scanning airplane) to Saudi Arabia in October 1981.[64]

Some legislative proposals have recommended that all executive agreements be subject to congressional veto. One of the earliest proponents of this view was Senator Sam Ervin. In 1972, 1973, and 1974, Ervin introduced one of the "most ambitious"[65] bills, requiring a sixty-day delay before any executive agreement entered into force; during this waiting period, both houses of Congress would have the opportunity to veto the agreement by a concurrent resolution. The Ervin bill passed the Senate in November 1974, only to die in the House without a vote.[66] Nonetheless, this initial legislation sparked an interest in the topic from other members of Congress. As a result, a spate of competing bills were proposed, debated in committee, and voted on the floor of Congress over the next four years.

Senator Lloyd Bentsen (D, Texas), for instance, re-introduced the Ervin bill in 1975 (S. 632).[67] Representative Gladys Spellman (D, Maryland) and Senator John Glenn (D, Ohio) also introduced identical bills in 1975 that would have allowed executive agreements to be vetoed by the Senate alone by simple resolution, following a sixty-day waiting period.[68] In the same year, Representative Thomas Morgan (D, Pennsylvania), then Chairman of the International Relations Committee (as the Foreign Affairs Committee was then called), introduced an-

A Second Resurgence

other bill (H.R. 4439) related to executive agreements, popularly known as the Morgan-Zablocki bill. In contrast to the previous proposals, only agreements that constituted a "national commitment" would be transmitted to Congress for the sixty-day review period. According to the proposed legislation, a "national commitment" meant any agreement or promise: "(1) regarding the introduction, basing, or deployment of the Armed Forces of the United States on foreign territory; or (2) regarding the provision to a foreign country, government, or people any military training or equipment including component parts and technology, any nuclear technology, or any financial or material resources."[69] While the Ervin, Bentsen, and Morgan proposals included both houses in the disapproval process, the Glenn and Spellman initiatives left the Senate with this responsibility. The rightful prerogatives of each chamber in the review of international agreements was rapidly becoming a tense issue on Capitol Hill.

The primary drawback of the congressional veto approach was that it invited delay and obstruction. Power is highly fragmented in the Congress; consequently, piecing together successful coalitions is time-consuming and frustrating. Failure is far more common than success. Moreover, the veto approach is a rather blunt instrument, capable of wiping out a broad and painstakingly devised agreement (say, military assistance to an entire region) when perhaps only a single aspect of the total package is unacceptable to the Congress (say, a specific weapons system going to a particular country). Such sweeping acts of congressional desperation could wreak havoc on the conduct of American foreign policy. Additionally, the thrust of the legislative veto approach put the burden to act upon the Congress rather than the executive. Why should the onus be placed upon the legislative branch to undertake the uphill political task of mobilizing a majority to stop an ill-conceived commitment initiated by the executive? If the executive branch has negotiated an important new commitment overseas, why should it not be required to achieve a positive majority vote on its own behalf in the Congress before the agreement takes effect? So, at least, reasoned those senators who favored a bolder approach to legislative control over agreement-making.

Majority approval. Focusing on the limited but important area of overseas military installations, Senator Case advanced the principle in 1973 that Congress should require positive legislative approval of such international commitments before they can be established—not just provide an opportunity to muster a difficult negative veto. Case attached an amendment to the Department of State authorization bill stating that no funds could be used to carry out any agreement establishing a military installation abroad until the agreement was approved either by a concurrent resolution of Congress or by the treaty process in the Senate. The amendment passed the Senate (S. 1248) and the conference committee, but the House rejected it.[70] In 1974, a similar amendment was added to the Department of State authorization bill (S. 3473), but was subsequently lost in conference.[71]

Treaty Powers Resolution. Stronger still was the remedy offered by Senator Dick Clark (D, Iowa) through his Treaty Powers Resolution, first introduced in April, 1976.[72] (See appendix C for a full text.) This legislation sought to express the sense of the Senate that any "significant" international agreement should be cast as a treaty and thus should be submitted to the Senate for its advice and consent.

Under the Clark proposal, the Senate Foreign Relations Committee would help the president determine whether a particular international agreement should be submitted as a treaty. Too often in the past, the executive branch has used its own solitary discretion in determining whether or not an agreement should be forwarded as a treaty. "According to the Constitution and [President Carter's] prerogatives as president," observed

A Second Resurgence

White House chief-of-staff, Hamilton Jordan, "[Carter] could present [the 1977 Panama Canal accord] to the Congress as a treaty, or as an agreement, and at the proper time he'll make that decision."[73] Senator Clark and his allies were sorely distressed by this "imbalance." As Clark remarked on the Senate floor during a key debate on the resolution:

> . . . under the existing situation, there is no balance. The President of the United States alone decides what is to be sent up as a treaty. The Senate has no choice in that whatsoever. If the President of the United States decides to send the SALT agreement to this body as a treaty, we will consider it as a treaty. If the President of the United States decides that it is an executive agreement, it will be an executive agreement. The Senate will not decide and will have no voice in that decision except insofar as the President may decide to consult with us.
>
> The same is true of any other international agreement. It is really, under the existing situation, the President, and the President alone, who decides whether any agreement that is signed is going to be considered by this body at all. The President can dispense with Senate advice and consent merely by calling a treaty an executive agreement. I do not see that as a fair balance.[74]

In 1970, the opinion of the Senate Foreign Relations Committee that the Spanish base agreement should have been submitted as a treaty was ignored by the executive branch. Now Senator Clark and company were out to settle the score.

Section 4 of the Treaty Powers Resolution bore sharp teeth: If the executive failed to submit an agreement that the Senate decided by resolution should have been submitted for ratification as a treaty, then the Senate rules would declare it henceforth out of order "to consider any bill or joint resolution or any amendment thereto, or any report of a committee of conference, which authorizes or provides budget authority to implement such international agreement."[75] The money spigots would remain shut off until the Senate gave its advice and consent to ratify the agreement in dispute.

141

The Democratic Control of International Agreements

A number of tangles in the Clark proposal were never worked out. First and foremost was the problem of definition. What kinds of agreements were "significant" enough to be treaties? Despite the difficulties, the proponents of the Clark Resolution needed to develop at least a rough set of guidelines to help delineate between significant international agreements and less important ones. These guidelines did not need to be (and probably could not be) definitive or set in concrete; at best, they would represent only the tentative opinions of a panel of experts. To a large extent, decisions would have to be particularistic, depending often upon the context; the rule of reason would have to be followed. In some cases disagreement might well—and properly so—lead to extended debate on the appropriate way to proceed, if the country were to make a commitment abroad.

Obviously, in the drafting of guidelines, quantitative rules alone would be insufficient. Who is to say whether $25 million or five hundred soldiers sent abroad mark the beginning of a "significant" commitment? Just one platoon of American marines sent to Africa or the Middle East could have a profound impact. An overriding principle for the establishment of guidelines might be that any new commitment or departure from existing policy would require the advice and consent of the Senate. (This should include "negative" decisions to end commitments—such as President Carter's disputed unilateral termination of the Taiwan Treaty by January 1, 1980[76]—as well as "positive" decisions to begin new ones.)

Whether a change in policy should go through the treaty procedure, become a statutory agreement, require some form of legislative resolution, or simply be accepted as an executive agreement would be a determination to be made by the Senate Foreign Relations Committee, or possibly the full Senate, under the terms of the Clark bill. But should the senators cry "treaty" while the president cries "executive agreement," the

A Second Resurgence

country could have a major debate on its hands—and perhaps, in particularly serious cases, a constitutional crisis as well. Certainly the executive branch was unhappy with the prospect of the Senate passing judgment on its choice of agreement instruments. The Department of State Legal Adviser for Treaty Affairs stressed to the Foreign Relations Committee during hearings on the Clark Resolution: ". . . there are some agreements that are concluded solely under the President's independent constitutional authority. The Congress may not constitutionally redesignate . . . such agreements as treaties."[77]

To permit an effective appraisal of international agreements by the Senate under a measure like the Treaty Powers Resolution, the executive branch would have to be required to submit more specific information about the anticipated nature of a commitment (as is now required for arms sales proposals). Approximate dollar estimates on the cost of a commitment, and an impact statement on its long-range implications, should supplement the present reporting requirements.[78] Furthermore, if an agreement were being negotiated pursuant to prior legislation, the executive should be required to provide more precise citations of prior legal authority. In this way, Congress could scrutinize the claim of authority and determine if its original decision is still valid and applicable (see chapter 6).

Although hearings were eventually held on the Clark proposal in 1976, no further action resulted. Evidently, the Senate was unwilling to endorse such a bold challenge to traditional executive prerogatives in the making of agreements abroad. In 1977, however, S. Res. 24, similar in construction to the original Clark proposal with the exception that agreements made pursuant to law or treaty were exempted, was again introduced.[79] Eventually, this proposal was incorporated as a section of the State Department Authorization Act in 1978 by the Senate Foreign Relations Committee and reported to the floor on a voice vote. Obviously, not even the Senate Foreign Relations Committee was wholly comfortable with the Treaty Powers Resolution; a Committee vote almost succeeded on May 10, 1978 (in a 7 to 7 tie) in removing the Treaty Powers Resolution from the bill.

On June 28, 1978, the floor debate on the resolution soon made it clear that a majority was probably unwilling to support this strong measure. Advocates of some form of a treaty-powers initiative turned to a substitute proposal offered by Senator Case. He explained his "less drastic" position to senators as they milled around the chamber: "This substitute requires consultation and provides the sanction that any agreement as to which the President does not consult the Senate shall be subject to a possible point of order in respect of implementation, instead of making any such agreement invalid in toto."[80] The veto of an executive agreement by the Senate thus would be less automatic, but sans consultation the threat remained with this substitute. The neo-insurgents now had their chance to vote on the basic principle behind the Clark Resolution: the right of prior consultation.

As the clerk called the roll, though, it was evident that the neo-insurgents were short on votes. The Case Substitute fell, 48 to 41.[81]

Next, Senator Glenn attempted to salvage some remnants of the treaty-powers principle with what he unabashedly admitted was a "fallback position," requiring simply that the executive branch "at least talk to us about what is proposed and whether it will be an executive agreement or a treaty." The former astronaut said he could "think of nothing more minimal than that."[82] His efforts at compromise read: "It is the sense of the Senate that, in determining whether a particular international agreement should be submitted as a treaty, the President should, prior to and during the negotiation of such agreement, seek the advice of the Committee on Foreign Relations as to whether it should be a treaty or an executive agreement." This language passed the Senate by voice vote, but was deleted in a Conference Committee meeting.[83]

A Second Resurgence

In retrospect, staff observers believe that these initiatives represented chiefly a "finger-shaking" exercise by the Senate Foreign Relations Committee toward the executive branch.[84] Ironically similar to the conservative Bricker amendment in its goal of limiting the authority of the president to commit the United States abroad, the Case Substitute—the strongest test of the treaty-powers proposal—was an initiative from a more liberal, Democratic, and Northeastern camp. Table 20 illustrates the differences in bases of support for the two rebellions.

Despite earlier setbacks, a new resolution, the International Agreement Consultation Resolution (S. Res. 536), was reported out of the Senate Foreign Relations Committee on August 25, 1978. It contained the same language as the Glenn substitute deleted in conference earlier.[85] The emergence of this resolution appeared to be the result of an agreement worked out on this issue in an exchange of letters between the Chairman of the Senate Committee, John Sparkman (D, Alabama), and the Assistant Secretary for Congressional Relations at the Department of State, Douglas J. Bennet, Jr.[86] Under the agreed-upon procedure, the Department of State would "inform the committee periodically, on a confidential basis, of significant international agreements which have been authorized for negotiation. . . ." In turn, the Committee would then advise the Department of State on any agreement that it would like to consult about further regarding the form the pact should take. Furthermore, Senator Sparkman asserted that this procedure "must cover all significant international agreements . . . regardless of the executive entity involved in the negotiation or approval processes."[87]

In the Senate report that reproduces these letters, the Foreign Relations Committee also stated several Senate prerogatives in the agreement process. First, the Committee expects that "*consultation*—not *notification*—will occur at any time an option is opened or foreclosed to use the treaty or executive agreement form in the case of any international agreement of

The Democratic Control of International Agreements

Table 20
A Comparison of Brickerites and Vietnam Insurgents by Party, Region, and Ideology

	Brickerites[a]		Vietnam Insurgents[a]	
	Pro (42)	Con (50)	Pro (41)	Con (48)
Party				
Democrat	13	33	30	23
Republican	29	17	11	36
Region[b]				
Northeast	6	15	15	7
South	10	16	8	16
Midwest	10	9	11	11
West	16	10	7	14
Ideology	2.4[c]	6.3	61[d]	30
	(11-point scale)		(100-point scale)	

[a] The key vote selected to distinguish core supporters of the Bricker movement was the February 25, 1954, vote on the Bricker Amendment (*Congressional Record*, p. 2262). For the Vietnam insurgents, a June 28, 1978, vote (the Case Substitute) was selected, since it represented the strongest test of the treaty-powers proposal (*Congressional Record*, p. 53076).

[b] The following standard grouping is used: Northeast—Maine, New Hampshire, Vermont, Massachusetts, Rhode Island, Connecticut, New York, New Jersey, Delaware, Maryland, Pennsylvania, West Virginia. South—Virginia, North Carolina, South Carolina, Georgia, Florida, Kentucky, Tennessee, Alabama, Mississippi, Arkansas, Louisiana, Oklahoma, Texas. Midwest—Ohio, Michigan, Indiana, Illinois, Wisconsin, Iowa, Minnesota, Missouri, North Dakota, South Dakota, Nebraska, Kansas. West—Montana, Idaho, Wyoming, Colorado, Utah, Nevada, New Mexico, Arizona, Washington, Oregon, California, Alaska, Hawaii.

[c] This liberal-conservative index is adapted from the ratings of the liberal magazine, *The New Republic* (October 11, 1954, supplement, p. 20). The magazine editors examined eleven votes for 1954 and gave each member a "+" if he or she demonstrated a "sound appraisal" on each vote (that is, voted the way the editors would have). Each "+" is scored as one point, on a scale running from 0 to 11. The figures in this table represent the mean score for proponents and opponents of the Bricker Amendment.

[d] These are scores prepared by the ADA (Americans for Democratic Action), a liberal group that rates legislators on a scale from 0 (conservative) to 100 (liberal). The scores are presented in Michael Barone, Grant Ujifusa, and Douglas Matthews, *The Almanac of American Politics 1980* (New York: E. P. Dutton, 1979).

significance, or at any time during negotiations at which either alternative becomes substantially more suitable" (emphasis added). Second, the word "advice" is used consciously in the resolution to underscore the Senate's constitutional role in the

A Second Resurgence

entire agreement process. Third, at the same time, the Committee grants that the Department of State can decide on what agreements to send forward. Trivial "or inconsequential agreements not subject to transmittal under the Case Act," would not need to be forwarded under this consultation arrangement. (See appendix D for the full texts of the two letters.)

With all of these "understandings" established, the full Senate approved S. Res. 536 on September 8, 1978.[88] The Senate had taken a major step toward enlarging its involvement in the agreement-making process—not as substantially as the original Clark Resolution or the Case Substitute had desired, nor even as much as the earlier Glenn or Bentsen proposals had sought, but more than it had ever taken before. The formula agreed upon fell short of strict legal constraints on the choices of forms by the executive branch for agreement-making, but demanded a more complete consultation between the branches on significant commitments abroad.

On the House side, though, members were apparently reluctant to place restraints on the executive branch in its conduct of international negotiations. The Morgan-Zablocki bill, for example, remained bottled up in committee. Still, the executive branch had been sent another strong message from the Senate: the less consultation from you, the more heat from us.

Internecine Warfare

Throughout these debates, the two chambers of Congress were often at one another's throats regarding the proper role of the House and the Senate in the approval of international agreements. Secretary of State John Foster Dulles noted in 1953 that an "undefined and probably undefinable borderline [exists] between international agreements which require two-thirds Senate concurrence, but no House concurrence, as in the case of treaties, and agreements which should have the majority concurrence of both chambers of Congress."[89] One thing was certain in these debates: members of the House, and especially the members of the House Foreign Affairs Committee, were increasingly eager, not to say avid, to play a part in reviewing international commitments. Their claim was based, in part, upon the constitutional budgetary authority provided to their chamber. This argument cannot be easily dismissed, in light of the millions of dollars that may be expended as a result of any treaty or less formal agreement.

The tension between the two chambers was clear in the contrasting language of the Senate-sponsored Treaty Powers Resolution and the House-sponsored Morgan-Zablocki Act. The House proposal provided both chambers with the right of disapproval within sixty days of "any executive agreement concerning the establishment, renewal, continuance, or revision of a national commitment." The Clark proposal excluded the House, but even more troubling to that chamber was Senator Clark's attack upon their bill in defense of his own. He called the Morgan-Zablocki bill a "clear invasion of the treaty process of the Senate. The authority to advise and consent to international agreements—or to refuse to do so—is conferred by the Constitution only on the Senate, not on the House of Representatives. . . . They [the Founding Fathers] envisaged a treaty-making process in which the Senate would operate, in the words of President Wilson, 'in the spirit of an executive council.' "[90] Additionally, the legal counsel to the Senate Foreign Relations Committee questioned the constitutionality of the Morgan-Zablocki bill. He claimed that the House bill would amend the Constitution by statute "by allowing the House to participate in advising and consenting to a certain class of international agreements under an alternate framework clearly in derogation of the treaty clause."[91]

Such an attack produced a rapid response by the House. This branch looks to the foreign commerce clause, the war power clause, and the "necessary and proper" clause of the Constitu-

A Second Resurgence

tion as a justification of its involvement. Members of the House appear to rely upon the power of the purse as their ultimate justification for their involvement over executive agreements. This point is well stated by one staff member of the House Foreign Affairs Committee: "Could the framers have intended otherwise than that the representatives of the taxpayers and citizens who must fulfill these national commitments, have a voice in this approval?"[92] Just as it is unjustifiable for the executive branch to enter into executive agreement in disregard of the Congress, similarly—according to the staff aide—it is unreasonable for the Senate to use the treaty power clause to deny legitimate House involvement in monitoring major international agreements. In short, the heart of this conflict is whether the House of Representatives should defer to the Senate treaty powers any more than both chambers should defer to the executive powers of the President.

Key members of the Senate Foreign Relations Committee, however, have been prepared to fight over this issue. "If they begin now to intrude on the treaty-making power of the Senate, we are going to find ourselves in a position where we can't do anything without the House's consent," observed Church, the ranking Democratic member of the Committee in 1977. "Their nibbles end up being big bites, and we being bitten to death."[93]

Almost two hundred years ago, Thomas Jefferson discussed this problem with President George Washington in reference to a proposed Algerian treaty. The Founding Fathers pondered what would happen if the House refused to appropriate funds to finance a treaty obligation enacted by the Senate. According to Jefferson's notes on the meeting, the President concluded that if the members of the House "would not do what the Constitution called on them to do, our government would be at an end, and must then assume another form."[94]

The internal bickering between chambers has delayed and

deflected the congressional challenge to executive power in the area of agreement-making. The executive branch is aware of the potential this dispute has for stalling any congressional action. A legal adviser for treaty affairs in the Department of State added fuel to the fire by commenting on the relative standing of the two Houses in these matters: "The Clark Resolution would constitute a very significant and unwise interference with the role of the House of Representatives. . . ."[95] In 1978, a situation somewhat the reverse of this problem—but nonetheless exacerbating this "between House" debate—captured the headlines: Should the ratification of the Panama Canal treaties by the Senate have allowed for the disposal of property in itself, or does the transfer of territory require House consent as well? Such questions serve to inflame this intramural controversy.

Vietnam Legacy

What then are we left with as a legacy of the second congressional revolt against insufficiently restrained agreement-making by the executive branch? After the countless individual expressions of dissatisfaction over presidential dominance, the hundreds of votes on bills and resolutions, and the scores of hearings, the statutory achievements toward the goal of a foreign-policy partnership must be judged as limited. While a few measures stand on the frontiers of this objective (such as the 1980 Intelligence Accountability Act), the end result in most policy areas has been the Case-Zablocki reporting requirement—tightened here and there to be sure, and a vast improvement over the pre-1972 era, but nevertheless a rudimentary stage in the series of proposals passed by the Senate at one time or another, but rejected by the House.

It would be wrong, however, to judge the executive-legislative balance in the agreement-making area by the passage of restraining laws alone. Accords like the one reached through an

A Second Resurgence

exchange of letters by Chairman Sparkman and the Department of State have helped to usher in a new mood of cooperation. Moreover, structural and procedural changes in foreign policy-making are likely to prevent inattention to Congress in the future. Its new committees (intelligence and budget, most notably), enlarged staffs, and expanded information sources (the Office of Technology Assessment, for one) provide Congress with vital instruments for monitoring affairs in the executive branch. Finally, Vietnam, Watergate, and the intelligence agency abuses remain sufficiently imprinted on the minds of enough legislators to preserve a continuing interest in congressional vigilance. More so than the Brickerites, because coming on the heels of harsher experiences, the neo-insurgents have shaken the foundations of foreign policy-making, from the war powers[96] to the treaty powers.

Ultimately, foreign policy commitments can determine where and when Americans must go to war. "If you've got children or grandchildren who might have to go," observed Senate minority leader Robert C. Byrd (D, West Virginia) recently, "you'd feel much better with Congress being brought in, than leaving it to one man."[97]

Notes

1. *Congressional Record*, February 2, 1954, p. 1106.
2. See, for example, William F. Buckley, Jr., "The CIA's $6 Million and Italian Politics," *Washington Star*, January 16, 1976.
3. Mrs. Robert Murray, Coordinator of the Vigilant Women for the Bricker Amendment, *Hearings*, S.J. Res. 1, Senate Judiciary Committee, 84th Congress, 1st Sess. (1955), p. 423.
4. Interview, February 21, 1970, Washington, D.C. See Loch Johnson, "Operational Codes and the Prediction of Leadership Behavior: Senator Frank Church at Mid-Career," in Margaret G. Herman, ed., *A Psychological Examination of Political Leaders* (New York: Free Press, 1977), pp. 80–119.
5. *Congressional Record*, February 26, 1954, p. 2372; *Congressional Record*, April 30, 1970, p. 13565.

6. Stephen A. Garrett, "Foreign Policy and the American Constitution: The Bricker Amendment in Contemporary Perspective," *International Studies Quarterly* 16 (June 1972), p. 213.

7. See testimony of undersecretary of state Nicholas Katzenbach, "U.S. Commitments to Foreign Powers," *Hearings*, Senate Foreign Relations Committee, 90th Cong., 1st Sess. (1967), p. 82.

8. *Congressional Record*, February 20, 1967, p. 3998.

9. Ibid., April 30, 1970, p. 13563.

10. Ibid., February 16, 1972, p. 4094. The language of the Case Act first appeared as part of the legislation offered by Senators Ferguson and Knowland in the fifties as an alternative to the Bricker amendment. See Gordon B. Baldwin, "Congressional Power to Demand Disclosure of Foreign Intelligence Agreements," *Brooklyn Journal of International Law* 3 (1967), pp. 6–7. This article provides an excellent review of the Case Act.

11. *Congressional Record*, August 14, 1972, p. 28087.

12. Pub.L. 92-403; 1 U.S.C., 1126 (1972).

13. "Transmittal of Executive Agreements to Congress," Senate Report No. 92-591, 92nd Cong., 2d Sess., January 19, 1972, p. 3.

14. Interview with senior staff member, House Committee on Foreign Affairs, October 7, 1982, Washington, D.C. See also David J. Kuchenbecker, "Agency-Level Executive Agreements: A New Era in U.S. Treaty Practice," *Columbia Journal of Transnational Law* 18 (1979), p. 42, a valuable source for the whole topic of executive agreements.

15. See Leslie H. Gelb, "A Domestic Challenge to Executive Agreements," *New York Times*, August 17, 1975.

16. Interviews with staff on the Senate Foreign Relations Committee and the House Foreign Affairs Committee, June 12 and 13, 1974, and October 7 and 8, 1982.

17. Cited in a report by the Comptroller General of the United States, *Reporting of U.S. International Agreements by Executive Agencies Has Improved*, October 31, 1978 (ID-78-57), p. 7.

18. Memorandum on "Late Executive Agreements," March 15, 1979.

19. Interview, May 28, 1974, Washington, D.C.

20. Interview, October 7, 1982, Washington, D.C.

21. Memo on "Late Executive Agreements."

22. 1 U.S.C. §112b, as amended by State Department Supplemental Appropriations Act of 1977 §5(a) Pub. L. No. 95–45, 91 Stat. 224 (1977).

23. Kuchenbecker, "Agency-Level Executive Agreements," p. 61.

24. Ibid., p. 64.

25. Ibid., p. 64, note 239.

26. Press release, office of Les Aspin, July 21, 1975. See Gelb, "Domestic Challenge to Executive Agreements."

27. Interview, staffer, House Select Committee on Intelligence, October 8, 1982, Washington, D.C. See also Arthur W. Rovine, "Separation of Pow-

A Second Resurgence

ers and International Executive Agreements," *Indiana Law Journal,* 52 (1977), p. 402, note 24; and "Reporting of U.S. International Agreements Has Improved," General Accounting Office report, October 31, 1978, p. 2. The most precise figures on this question indicate the reporting of 63 classified agreements to the two foreign affairs committees between August 22, 1972 (when Case-Zablocki went into effect) and March 29, 1977. Letter from Arthur W. Rovine, Assistant Legal Adviser for Treaty Affairs, Department of State, to Michael Glennon, Counsel, Senate Committee on Foreign Relations, March 29, 1977.

28. Gelb, "Domestic Challenge to Executive Agreements."
29. Interview, June 12, 1974, Washington, D.C.
30. Interview, staffer, House Select Committee on Intelligence, November 28, 1978, Washington, D.C.
31. Report of the Comptroller General of the United States, "U.S. Agreements with the Republic of Korea," ID-76-20 (February 20, 1976), p. 8.
32. Joseph S. Nye, Jr., "Independence and Interdependence," *Foreign Policy* 22 (Spring 1976), p. 138.
33. Raymond Hopkins, "The International Role of 'Domestic' Bureaucracy," *International Organization* 30 (1976), p. 424.
34. See Kuchenbecker, "Agency-Level Executive Agreements," pp. 11, 55 (note 193), 56.
35. Ibid., pp. 1, 48, 49.
36. Letter to Secretary of Defense James Schlesinger (September 6, 1973), reprinted in "Congressional Oversight of Executive Agreements—1975," *Hearings,* Subcommittee on Separation of Powers, Senate Committee on the Judiciary, 94th Cong., 1st Sess., 1975, pp. 101–102. See also "Congressional Review of International Agreements," *Hearings,* Subcommittee on International Security and Scientific Affairs, House Committee on International Relations, 94th Cong., 2nd Sess., June and July 1976, pp. 244–45.
37. See Rovine, "Separation of Powers," p. 404; and Kuchenbecker, "Agency-Level Executive Agreements," p. 44.
38. See Monroe Leigh, "Case Act Procedures and Department of State Criterion for Deciding What Constitutes an International Agreement," reprinted in "Congressional Review of International Agreements," *Hearings,* Subcommittee on International Security and Scientific Affairs, House Committee on International Relations, 94th Cong., 2d Sess., June and July 1976, pp. 240–43.
39. E. C. McDowell, *Digest of U.S. Practices in International Law,* 1976, p. 263; and Kuchenbecker, "Agency-Level Executive Agreements," pp. 13–14.
40. Kuchenbecker, "Agency-Level Executive Agreements," p. 15.
41. Interview with Marjorie Ann Browne, Congressional Research Service, Library of Congress, October 6, 1982, Washington, D.C.
42. Robert L. Bridge, "The New Air Force International Agreement Pro-

cedure," *The Reporter* (Office of the Judge Advocate General of the Air Force) 5 (August 1978), p. 22. Also see *Reporting on U.S. International Agreements Has Improved*, General Accounting Office report, pp. 14–18, on DOD procedures and compliance.

43. "Future Commitments to Foreign Governments," Memorandum, to the Secretaries of State, Treasury, and Defense; the Director, OMB; and the Assistant to the President for National Security Affairs, April 15, 1977.

44. Letter to Cyrus Vance, November 30, 1977, reprinted in "Foreign Relations Authorization Act, FY 1979," Senate Foreign Relations Committee Report No. 95-842, 95th Cong., 2d Sess., May 15, 1978, p. 46. See also Kuchenbecker, "Agency-Level Executive Agreements," p. 65.

45. Pub. L. 95-426; 95 Stat. 933.

46. Kuchenbecker, "Agency-Level Executive Agreements," p. 68.

47. Marjorie Ann Browne, *Executive Agreements and the Congress*, Issue Brief Number IB 75035, Washington, D.C.: Congressional Research Service, February 27, 1981, p. 5. This source is valuable for a brief summary of congressional action in the agreement-making area.

48. Part VII, 1977, p. 11. These procedures remain in effect. The phrase "executive agreement" in section one is used broadly in the *Manual* to include statutory and executive agreements, as defined in this study.

49. Interview, Washington, D.C., June 23, 1974.

50. Interview, Washington, D.C., June 24, 1974. Perhaps he should be happy; sleeping dogs don't bite.

51. Interview, Washington, D.C., May 4, 1977.

52. Quoted by James Reston, "Bewildered Congress Faces World Leadership Decision," *New York Times*, March 14, 1947.

53. Loch Johnson, "Legislative Reform of Intelligence Policy," paper presented at the International Studies Association, South, annual meeting, Atlanta, Georgia, November 6, 1982.

54. Arguably, the CIA interpretation was a self-serving misrepresentation of the original intent of Hughes-Ryan. According to one of the original co-sponsors and floor leaders during the debate on Hughes-Ryan, inclusion of an earlier phrase "unless and until" in the act required "prior notice" to the Congress. See John L. Burton (D, California), who added this earlier phrase himself, *Congressional Record*, September 30, 1980, p. H10047. The exception occurred in 1979 when the CIA took longer than its normal period to inform the intelligence committees about an operation with the Canadian embassy in Iran designed, successfully, to spirit away a few fortunate American diplomats there who otherwise no doubt would have been captured and taken hostage with the rest of the American embassy personnel.

55. As part of the Intelligence Authorization Act, *Congressional Record*, September 19, 1980, p. S12959.

56. See Loch Johnson, "The U.S. Congress and the CIA: Monitoring the

A Second Resurgence

Dark Side of Government," *Legislative Studies Quarterly* 5 (November 1980), pp. 477–99.

57. July 22, 1981.
58. Interview with staff member, June 14, 1983.
59. Interview with staff director, October 8, 1982.
60. Another of the few laws with these provisions is the Fishery Conservation Management Act of 1976 (P. L. 94-265), which requires that the text of each international agreement in the fishery area be submitted to Congress sixty days prior to the effective date of the agreement.
61. "Studies on the Legislative Veto," prepared by the Congressional Research Service for the Committee on Rules, House of Representatives, Committee Print, February 1980, p. 1.
62. "Congress and Foreign Policy," Special Subcommittee on Investigations, report, 1977, p. 10. In *Immigration and Naturalization Service v. Chadha* (June 23, 1983), the Supreme Court declared the Congressional veto unconstitutional. Congress is now working through the meaning of this decision for the hundreds of affected statutes. See I. M. Destler, "Dateline Washington: Life After the Veto," *Foreign Policy* 52 (Fall 1983), pp. 181–86.
63. See "Executive-Legislative Consultation on Foreign Policy: Strengthening the Legislative Side," House Foreign Affairs Committee Print, prepared by the Congressional Research Service (Congress and Foreign Policy Series no. 5), April 1982, pp. 61–62.
64. See Pub. L. 93-559 for the Nelson-Bingham Amendment and Pub. L. 94-329 (the International Security Assistance and Arms Export Control Act of 1976) for the revisions in Nelson-Bingham. The information on the informal notification arrangement was obtained from an interview with a Department of State official, Washington, D.C., October 1981. The setting of cost ceilings to trigger executive branch reporting can be tricky. The $7 million ceiling excluded the controversial proposal to sell relatively inexpensive but highly destabilizing concussion bombs to Israel, first approved secretly by President Ford, then leaked, and subsequently disapproved by President Carter.
65. John B. Rehm, "Making Foreign Policy Through International Agreement," in Francis O. Wilcox and Richard A. Frank, eds., *The Constitution and the Conduct of Foreign Policy* (New York: Praeger, 1976), p. 131.
66. Senate Report No. 93-1286, 93d. Cong., 2d Sess., 1974.
67. *Congressional Record*, February 7, 1975.
68. Ibid., March 20, 1975 (H.R. 5489 and S. 1251).
69. Ibid., March 6, 1975, quote from p. 4 of the bill.
70. *Congressional Record*, September 11, 1973, p. H.7727.
71. "State Department, USIA Authorizations," House Report No. 93-1447, 93d Cong., 2d Sess., October 8, 1974, pp. 13–14. The 1983 Supreme Court ruling would prohibit the concurrent resolution form of "veto."
72. S. Res. 434, later reintroduced in revised form in July 1976 as S. Res.

486. For S. Res. 434, see the *Congressional Record*, April 14, 1976, p. 10966; for S. Res. 486, see the *Congressional Record*, July 1, 1976, p. 22078.

73. "Face the Nation," CBS News, November 12, 1978.

74. *Congressional Record*, 95th Cong., 2d Sess., June 28, 1978, p. S10010.

75. S. Res. 486, 94th Cong., 2d Sess.

76. On July 6, 1979, the Senate rebuked President Carter for ending the mutual defense treaty with Taiwan, without Senate consultation, by voting 59 to 35 in a sense-of-the-Senate resolution that such a far-reaching decision should require Senate consent. See Bernard Gwertzman, "Senate Rebukes Carter Over Ending of Taiwan Pact," *New York Times*, June 7, 1979. Earlier, the Federal District Court came close to siding with the Congress ("the power to terminate treaties is a power shared by the political branches of this government," said Judge Oliver Gasch, "namely the President and the Congress"), but ultimately declined on technical grounds. The Supreme Court, however, was overwhelmingly unsympathetic to Congress; by a vote of 7 to 2, the Court held on December 13, 1979, that the President had the constitutional authority to terminate the Taiwan defense pact unilaterally. On this case, *Goldwater v. Carter* [444 U.S. 996 (1979)], see Michael J. Glennon, "Treaty Process Reform: Saving Contitutionalism Without Destroying Diplomacy," *University of Cincinnati Law Review* 52 (1983), pp. 84–107; and Richard Carell, "Way Cleared for Ending of Taiwan Pact," *Washington Post*, December 14, 1979.

77. "Treaty Powers Resolution," *Hearings*, Committee on Foreign Relations, U.S. Senate, 94th Cong., 2d Sess., July 21 and 28, 1976 (Washington, D.C.: U.S. Government Printing Office, 1977), p. 83.

78. On impact statements in the arms-control area, see George Berdes, "Congress' New Leverage," *The Center Magazine*, July/August 1976, pp. 76–80; and "Executive-Legislative Consultation," House Foreign Affairs Committee Print, April 1982, pp. 51–53.

79. *Congressional Record*, January 10, 1977, p. S342.

80. *Congressional Record*, June 28, 1978, p. S10004. The text of the Case Substitute is at pp. S10003–04.

81. Ibid., p. S10009.

82. Ibid., p. S100012. The text of the Glenn compromise is on the same page.

83. *Congressional Quarterly Almanac 1978*, (Washington, D.C.: Congressional Quarterly Press, 1979), p. 414.

84. Interviews, June 28, 1978, Washington, D.C.

85. "International Agreements Consultation Resolution," Senate Report No. 95-1171, 95th Cong., 2d Sess., August 25, 1978.

86. Ibid., pp. 2–3.

87. Ibid., p. 2.

88. *Congressional Record*, 95th Cong., 2d Sess., 1978, p. 28545.

A Second Resurgence

89. "Treaties and Executive Agreements," *Hearings*, Subcommittee of the Judiciary Committee, U.S. Senate, 82nd Cong., 2d Sess., p. 21.

90. *Congressional Record*, 94th Cong., 2d Sess., 1976, p. S5745. On the demise of this "executive council" concept, see Louis Henkin, *Foreign Affairs and the Constitution* (Mineola, New York: Foundation Press, 1972), p. 131.

91. Michael J. Glennon, "Remarks on the Panel on Treaties and Executive Agreements," presented at the annual meeting of the American Society of International Law, San Francisco, April 23, 1977, p. 5 (mimeo).

92. James T. Schollaert, "A Critique of Recent U.S. Practice of International Agreements Law," paper presented at the annual meeting of the American Society of International Law, San Francisco, April 23, 1977, p. 4 (mimeo).

93. *Hearings*, Committee on Foreign Relations, U.S. Senate, 95th Cong., 1st Sess., 1977, p. 21.

94. *Writings of Jefferson* (Ford, ed.), vol. i, p. 191. MSS *Jefferson Papers*, series 4, vol. ii, no. 36.

95. Rovine, "Separation of Powers," p. 428.

96. On this important side of the congressional revolution, see Barbara Hinkson Craig, "The Power to Make War: Congress' Search for an Effective Role," *Journal of Policy Analysis and Management* 1 (1982), pp. 317–33.

97. *New York Times*, September 21, 1983.

6.

A Foreign Policy Partnership

> In an age of nuclear weapons, when issues of war and peace require an executive capable of prompt and vigorous action, they also pose risks far too great for the nation to vest decision-making authority in the hands of one man or a few men at the pinnacle of executive power. It is the task of Congress to resolve this dilemma by maintaining an institutional balance of power which disciplines the President without paralyzing him.
>
> —ALTON FRYE, *The Responsible Congress*

A New Era

Surely the first rule of international agreement-making in a democracy is that foreign commitments—if they are to be sustained—must rest upon the consent of the public. The thesis of this study is straightforward: although the Congress has participated in the making of many international agreements, major commitments—especially in the military and intelligence areas—have been decided by the president alone or, worse still, by non-elected officials in the executive branch. The president

A Foreign Policy Partnership

needs help from other elected officials in the federal government; members of Congress need to review American commitments in a more meaningful way.

Congress may be seen as an assembly of public policy specialists. By interest, training, or committee experience, some members have specialized in foreign policy. Legislation like the Treaty Powers Resolution seeks to interject these congressional experts into the process by which the United States establishes, or withdraws from, obligations in other lands. Further, the Congress provides more than just another arena of expertise; even more important is its sensitivity to public opinion and what might be acceptable to the American people. Why should the president and his assistants alone decide what is legitimately an executive agreement or a treaty, what is trivial or significant, what should be done quietly or with full debate? In a democracy, should not both the Congress and the executive branch play a part in this important process?

The author is under no illusion that the republic will be saved from errors of judgment by the Senate Foreign Relations Committee or the House Foreign Affairs Committee. One is aware that sometimes members of Congress have behaved irresponsibly in the handling of foreign affairs. Particularly deplorable are those occasions when members attempt to legislate hastily on the floor, without allowing appropriate committees to study and debate policy through the regular process of staff research and thorough hearings. The executive branch, with its vast information resources and competent diplomatic advisers, must be allowed to present its case in full. Unfortunate, too, are those instances when individual members of Congress have promoted themselves to the office of Secretary of State. A single secretary of state is sufficient; 536 promise chaos. One can only remember with dismay the spectacle of Representative George V. Hansen (R, Idaho) rushing off to Teheran in 1979 to try to negotiate the release of American hostages.

The Democratic Control of International Agreements

Neither, however, can one be comforted by a presidency omniscient, omnipresent, and omnipotent in foreign policy-making. Both institutions are human, and, therefore, both are fallible. The nation's best hope lies in the wisdom each is able to bring to common problems facing the nation. It is this pooling of information, ideas, experience, judgment, and awareness of public sentiment that should be espoused. Here is the best remedy against the most tragic lesson history has to teach, that unlimited power in the hands of a single person or institution holds great danger to the citizenry. A foreign policy partnership between the legislative and executive branches provides the best safeguard against this aggrandizement.

For the more effective conduct of foreign policy, the United States requires an executive-legislative compact, as envisaged by Warren Christopher (who served as undersecretary of state during the Carter administration). "As a fundamental precept," he writes, "the compact would call for restraint on the part of the Congress—for Congress to recognize and accept the responsibility of the Executive to conduct and manage foreign policy on a daily basis." He properly stresses that the executive branch must be prepared to provide Congress "full information and consultation," and "broad policy should be jointly designed." For its part, Congress should only rarely, in extreme circumstances, attempt "to dictate or overturn Executive decisions and actions. . . ."[1] The challenge is to strike this proper balance.

Full participation by both branches may lead at times to controversy, and even confrontation. The many books and articles on executive-legislative relations usually recommend greater consultation and comity (the favorite word of constitutional scholars), not new laws and procedures, to ease the institutional tension. This sounds like a reasonable suggestion; certainly no one is against the idea of the executive branch consulting more with the Congress and developing friendlier

A Foreign Policy Partnership

relations. The trouble with this informal approach, however, is that it often fails to work.

"In the interest of orderly procedures," opined John Foster Dulles when he was Secretary of State, "I feel that the Congress is entitled to know the considerations that enter into the determinations as to which procedures are sought to be followed. To that end, when there is any serious question of this nature and circumstances permit, the executive branch will consult with appropriate congressional leaders and committees in determining the most suitable way of handling international agreements as they arise."[2] Yet the Congress was only inconsistently consulted in the fifties (certainly infrequently by Dulles), and it has been sporadically ignored in the subsequent three decades. That is why many members of the legislative branch want to go beyond a hit-or-miss reliance on occasional consultations and feelings of comity to develop a more formal, systematic, and reliable reporting and reviewing procedure for international agreements. As William Diebold, Jr. has aptly noted, "It will be prudent for the Executive to keep in close touch with Congress, which feels about the fait accompli much as nature does about vacuums."[3]

As this book illustrates, a continuum of approaches is available to the executive branch in the making of international agreements. This ranges, on one end, from complete executive discretion by way of secret verbal or written assurances to another country (such as Nixon's promise of aid to North Vietnam or various intelligence agreements) to, on the other end, commitments made through the formal treaty process with Senate participation (obvious examples are the NATO Treaty and the Nuclear Test Ban Treaty). It is the gray middle area between executive authority and institutional sharing that has been particularly disputable to those seeking limits to executive discretion.

The controversy surrounding the Sinai agreements of Sep-

The Democratic Control of International Agreements

tember 1975 between the United States, Israel, and Egypt demonstrates this middle-range difficulty. These agreements established an early warning system to help keep the Mideast peace and called for American technicians to assist in its operations. The agreements became controversial because some members of Congress believed they should have taken the form of treaties, since they involved American personnel in an area of potential future conflict. The executive branch argued through the State Department Legal Adviser for Treaty Affairs, however, that the president "is expected to adhere to the customs and practices which have developed since the conclusion of the first executive agreements." But, ". . . the President has the discretion to choose whether to conclude any particular agreement as a treaty or as an executive agreement."[4]

Perhaps because of the controversy surrounding the placement of American technicians in a war-ready zone, the executive branch ultimately backed away from the discharge of this commitment solely by executive authority. In the final text of the Sinai accords, President Ford wrote to the presidents of Israel and Egypt that "as soon as the Congress of the United States has given its approval to United States participation in the Early Warning System, I will notify you, and this proposal shall be regarded as an agreement between us."[5] What some wanted to be a treaty and others an executive agreement finally became a statutory agreement in order for the Congress to give its approval to the commitment.

Yet perhaps with the precedent of the Gulf of Tonkin resolution in mind, the legislators refused to grant open-ended language in their approval. The Sinai resolution specified that the congressional authorization of American technicians in the Middle East did not imply approval of any other agreement, understanding, or commitment that might have been made at the same time, secretly or verbally, by the executive branch. Congress, moreover, required the president to submit reports at least every

A Foreign Policy Partnership

six months, so long as the American technicians were still on duty, on the scope and duration of their participation.[6]

As the Sinai example suggests, disagreements will continue to arise over the appropriate form that international agreements should take. No doubt Senator Bricker was correct when he said that "it is probably impossible to draw a satisfactory line of demarcation even in a statute" between treaties and executive agreements.[7] Most members of Congress, however, seem less concerned today with the establishment of a fine and everlasting dichotomy between these two forms of agreement-making than they are with gaining assurances that the Congress will be informed about international agreements, and provided adequate opportunity to judge whether a commitment is sufficiently important to deserve broader congressional participation in the decision-making process (either through a treaty or some other form of legislative involvement).

The judgment here is that virtually all international agreements, from verbal promises (which should be used only rarely) to open, written agreements, ought to be reported to the Congress early enough to allow serious congressional appraisal before the commitment is sealed. Executive privilege must extend to these discussions, just as it does to talks between the president and his aides, if we are to have frank and meaningful relations with other countries. Once general discussions reach a stage of promised commitments, however, our diplomatic negotiators and representatives should be obliged to make it known that whatever commitments are agreed upon, oral or written (in contrast to the free exploration of options and possibilities), must be communicated to the Congress. If the commitments are of a sensitive nature, they will be protected in both branches under secrecy provisions, as has been the rule under the Case-Zablocki Act.

Senator Humphrey told Secretary of State Cyrus Vance on the eve of his trip to the Middle East in 1977: "Don't make any

The Democratic Control of International Agreements

commitments until you've been back here [to Congress]—not even smiling ones."[8] It is not a matter of violating executive privilege, but of who can genuinely commit the United States to what. Here members of the Congress believe they have a legitimate right to participate, and they know that a prerequisite for participation is an awareness of executive branch intentions.

Recommendations

In pursuit of enhanced legislative participation, this volume closes with five policy recommendations.

Computer Monitoring of International Agreements

If Congress is serious about monitoring commitments made by the United States abroad, its foreign policy committees must equip themselves with modern technology to perform this task effectively. Congress already has an impressive infrastructure for information processing. Hundreds of staffers use more than two thousand computer terminals presently in operation on Capitol Hill.[9] What must be done now is to direct available facilities toward assisting legislators and their aides in the tracking of international agreements. Sophisticated information storage and retrieval systems are vastly more effective and flexible than paper files.

Given the excellent systems already in place, this objective involves minimal expense and technical difficulty; the essential necessary condition is a determination to proceed in this direction by legislators on the appropriate committees (at a minimum, the Senate Foreign Relations Committee and the House Foreign Affairs Committee). Despite its acceptance of computers for bibliographic searches in the Library of Congress, for reports on the status of bills, and a few other tasks, Congress (as Stephen E. Frantzich notes) "has not taken advantage of the

A Foreign Policy Partnership

computer to improve its oversight functions by independently monitoring the effectiveness of enacted legislation."[10]

Are the foreign policy committees ready now to replace committee memory and bulging file cabinets with efficient computer storage and retrival of agreements reported under the Case-Zablocki Act? If so, two steps are required, one in-house and the other in cooperation with the executive branch.

The in-house requirement involves the simple expansion of an existing congressional computer aid called SCORPIO (subject-content–oriented retriever for processing information online). Developed by the Information Systems Office in the Library of Congress, SCORPIO is a computer language that allows the user to frame inquiries and receive answers by video display or printed response. At present, a dozen data files are accessible through the SCORPIO language, a data file being simply an organized collection of information oriented toward some purpose—such as listing all the books held by the Library of Congress since 1969, as does one of the existing files. Other SCORPIO files contain information on the status of bills (with the names of sponsors, a selected chronology, digests, and the like); synopses of over two hundred major issues before the Congress; a periodical catalogue, with over 100,000 citations; and a listing of over ten thousand organizations and people willing and able to respond to questions on almost any topic (the National Referral Center Resources File).

For the purpose of monitoring international agreements, the Congress could establish an additional SCORPIO file for this policy area (and, for that matter, files for oversight responsibilities on other topics, such as the compilation of status reports on environmental clean-ups). Mechanically, the initial task would be to decide what information about international agreements the Congress wished to have reported by the executive branch. Among the most helpful items of information would be the expected financial cost of the agreement; whether the agreement represents a radical departure from previous policy; the target country; the form of the agreement; the statutory or constitutional authority; the subject matter (military bases, for example); and the dates of signing and effectiveness.

The various executive agencies engaged in agreement-making would be responsible for gathering this information, all using the same standard form (or "input format," in computer terminology). These forms would then be forwarded to the Department of State, which would clear the agreement and send on to the Congress copies of the approved forms. (See figure 6 for a proposed input format). There, a staff computer program-

Figure 6
International Agreement Reporting Form (Case-Zablocki Act Input Format)

1. Nations or international organizations party to the agreement:	8. Date signed:
	9. Effective date:
	10. Expected year of termination:
2. Reporting agency:	11. Agency reference number:
3. Subject of agreement:	12. State Department reference number:
4. Agreement form:	
5. Source of authority (specify U.S. code, if applicable):	13. Date reported to State Department:
6. Estimated costs:	14. Date approved by State Department:
7. New or continuing policy (specify which):	15. Date reported to Congress:
16. Agency reporting official: Phone number:	17. State Department reporting official: Phone number:
18. Comments:	19. *For congressional use* Date of entry into SCORPIO: Programmer: Comments:

mer (perhaps one shared by the two foreign affairs committees) would simply enter this data into the new SCORPIO file (the International Agreements file).

By way of programming, for example, three numerical columns in the International Agreements file could be reserved for the subject matter of the agreement, as illustrated below:

001 = military bases
016 = tariff agreements
021 = protection of migratory birds
990 = international control of injurious insects

Figure 7 suggests a codebook for the entry of agreement data into the new SCORPIO file.

This approach would allow Congress to store and analyze international agreements in a quick, efficient, and sophisticated way. Most importantly, the foreign affairs committees could program their computer terminals to "kick out" for special attention agreements that seem to be of major importance or risk. This procedure would not eliminate individual members of Congress and staff who might want to scrutinize all the agreements on a regular basis. It would assist, however, those members and staffers too occupied with other matters to focus on all commitments abroad. Every agreement that cost, say, over $200,000, dealt with military matters, claimed pure constitutional authority, or represented a totally new policy direction could be easily sorted out by the machine. The thousands of routine agreements would be routinely stored in the computer and held for close staff scrutiny. Key commitments could then be brought to the attention of the legislators. With members and staff too busy to do the job, the computer would be responsible for raising a red flag to draw the attention of Congress toward those commitments that warrant thorough debate.

With this new computer file, it would be possible to obtain quick answers to such questions as: How many agreements do

Figure 7
Illustrative Codebook for the Reporting of International Agreements Under the Case-Zablocki Act

Items	Computer Code
Initials of reporting agency officer	KEJ
Telephone contact number	303-548-9666
Initials of reporting State Department officer	LKJ
Telephone contact number	202-548-9653
Reporting agency	16 (Defense Department)
Subject matter	014 (military base)
Target nation (or international entity)	078 (Taiwan)
Agreement form	3 (executive agreement)
Authority (insert U.S. code citation, if applicable)	00000000000000000000-000001 (Constitution)
Estimated costs	001,000,000 ($1 million)
Date of signing	011283 (1 December 1983)
Date of effectiveness	010384 (1 March 1984)
Date of agency reporting to State Department	041283 (4 December 1983)
Date of State Department reporting to Congress	061283 (6 December 1983)
New or continuing policy	2 (continuing)
Expected year of agreement termination	99 (indefinite)
State Department reference number	5487796

we have with Israel? With Saudi Arabia? What agreements are scheduled to end this year? How many agreements allowing the establishment of American forces overseas have been negotiated in the past three years? With what nations?

This capability would allow those individuals screening new agreements to find related or similar agreements quickly, and thorough retrospective studies would become feasible. (Executive officials involved in the negotiation or review of international agreements could be provided access to this sophisticated reservoir of data.) Naturally, classified agreements could not be stored in a SCORPIO file; such information, however,

A Foreign Policy Partnership

could be held in small computers located in the vaults of the two intelligence committees, with appropriate measures taken to protect the computers from electronic monitoring.

In summary, the information required by Congress could be easily provided on a standard form by the agency negotiating an agreement, sent to the Department of State for review, then forwarded to the congressional committees for insertion into SCORPIO—all with greater dispatch and usefulness than under current procedures. By requiring the Department of State to put the agreements in standard form, another roadblock would be placed in the way of the executive branch, forcing it to be more sensitive to congressional prerogatives in making agreements abroad. In short, the Department of State would likely become more reluctant to rely solely on executive authority in making foreign commitments.

The end result, then, would be an electronic library on international agreements, providing early and automatic alert on important commitments, quickly retrievable agreement "profiles," and easy listing (say, all the military agreements with African nations in 1983) or analytic manipulation of these data. Without great difficulty the committee programmer could enter into the SCORPIO file all past international agreements, which would eventually provide the Congress with a rich longitudinal data base to assist its judgment of proposed commitments abroad.

After establishing the SCORPIO file, the second essential step is to achieve executive branch cooperation with the new reporting format. This should be simple enough, as the proposed form is similar to the standard fare for much executive branch reporting. It should, in fact, simplify reporting on agreements by making more precise what the Congress wishes to know (though cost estimates may be hard or impossible to predict exactly on some agreements).

The use of a SCORPIO file by Congress for recording inter-

The Democratic Control of International Agreements

national agreements represents a so-called "pointing system," wherein a computer is used to retrieve information that is indexed (in this case, by date of signing, subject, agreement form, and the rest). The index in turn points to an actual document (here, an international agreement) stored outside the computer (in the *Treaties and Other International Agreement Series*, or TIAS, which are printed volumes). Such systems are analogous to card catalogues used in libraries, where the call numbers point to the location of the books. In contrast, a "full-text system," as the name implies, provides the verbatim text of the document within the computer.[11] These systems are expensive, for they involve the storage of massive amounts of data.

Both types of systems would be useful to Congress in its monitoring of foreign commitments. The SCORPIO file would allow easy retrieval of agreements data according to key specified categories (indices). The full-text system would provide a powerful tool for a thorough search of agreement language. One might want to retrieve every agreement in which the word "Israel" is mentioned, or "AWACS," or "deep-water ports." The scope and flexibility of this full-text option is great, and is widely used in the legal profession for case searching.

Just as the adaptation of SCORPIO for the monitoring of agreements is a manageable task, so, too, is the linkage of Congress to a full-text system containing all international agreements. On October 9, 1974, a Department of Defense Directive (No. 5160.64) established a full-text system containing all international agreements printed in TIAS (as well as other legal documents). Called FLITE (federal legal information through electronics), the system is operated by the Department of the Air Force for use by all federal agencies. So far, Congress has failed to take advantage of access to this bank of complete agreement texts.

By telephoning the FLITE offices in Denver, Colorado, congressional committees—were they to become subscribers to

A Foreign Policy Partnership

this service—could request full-text searches according to key words or expressions in international agreements. The results would then be delivered overnight in a batch to the Congress. This "batch processing" no doubt will be supplemented one day by an "on-line" FLITE capability, allowing committees to have a continuing communications hook-up with FLITE offices and to refine search commands as a search proceeds.

The flow chart in figure 8 suggests in schematic form how the tracking of international agreements could be facilitated by the use of SCORPIO and FLITE procedures. The executive branch, like the rest of our society, is moving toward the acceptance of paperless information systems. If it is to perform its Madisonian mandate as a check upon the executive, Congress will find it increasingly necessary to adopt contemporary technological innovations for this difficult but essential responsibility.

Prior Notification

To allow legislators a chance to review commitments abroad, the core information on agreements outlined above should be submitted to Congress sixty days prior to the date when the agreement is supposed to go into effect (except in emergency cases). This would permit the fruitful consultation envisaged in the Sparkman-Bennet letters of 1978 (discussed in chapter 5; see appendix D for the letters).

Audits

Sample audits, like the 1976 GAO probe into United States–Korean agreements (see chapter 3), should be conducted in different countries each year. Also, the GAO (and, ideally, if properly staffed, the Department of State) should peek into the agency closets now and then to check on agreement-reporting fidelity. Legal specialists on the staff of the Congressional Research Service, moreover, might be delegated to ex-

Figure 8
A Systems Flowchart for the Monitoring of Reporting on International Agreements under the Case-Zablocki Act

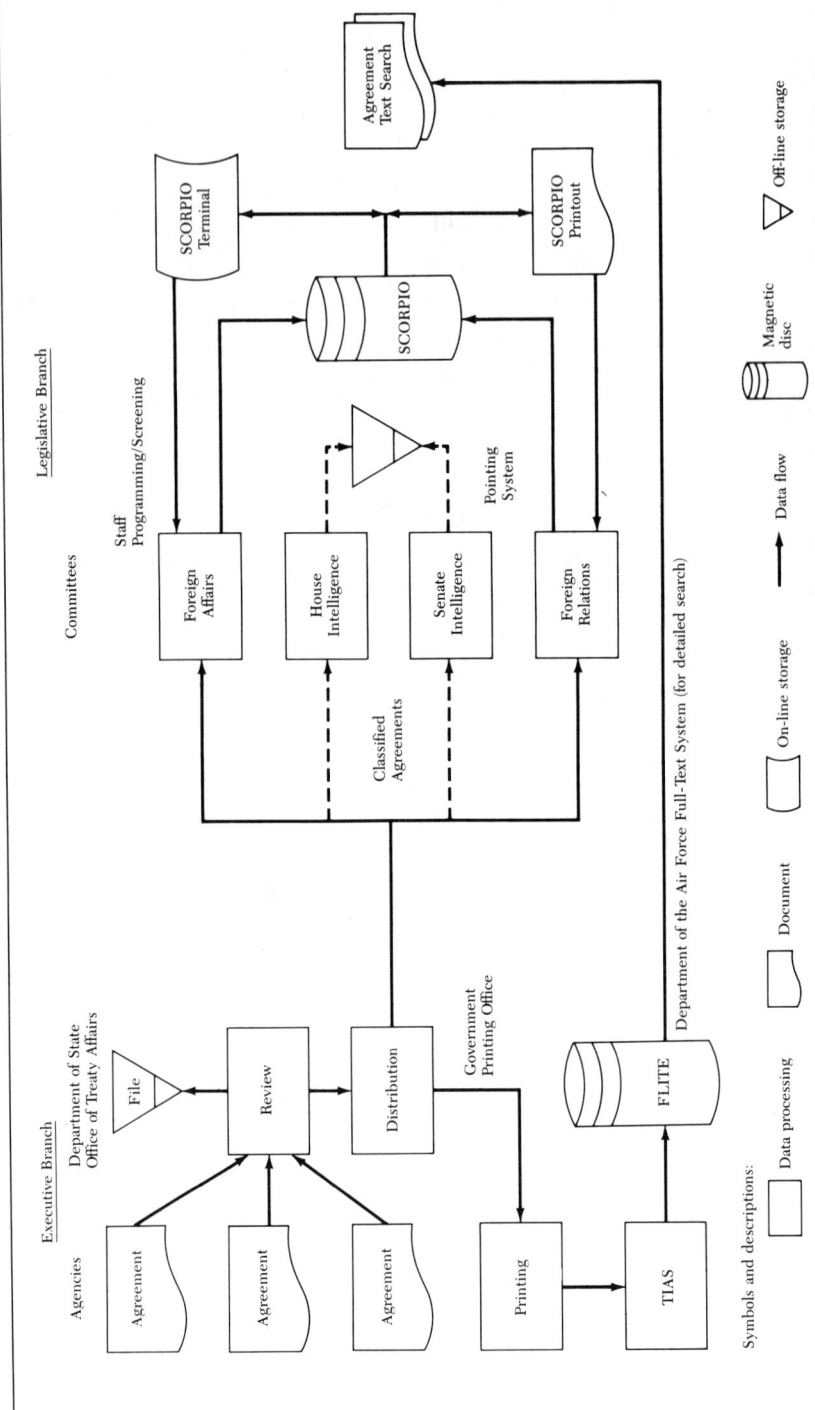

NOTE: Symbols adapted from International Organization for Standardization (ISO) International Standard 1028, "Information Processing—Flowchart Symbols" and American National Standard, "Flowchart Symbols and Their Usage in Information Processing," ANSI X3.5-1970.

amine the accuracy of executive branch claims to legislative authority in a random sample of recent statutory agreements.[12]

Enhanced Reporting Standards

As David J. Kuchenbecker recommends, an executive order from the president would be useful to direct the federal bureaucracy toward tightening up its record-keeping and reporting on agency-level agreements.[13] Such an order could also be used to inaugurate the proposed new reporting format.

Comprehensive Review of the Agreement-Making Process

This study supports the call for a full legislative review of the procedures by which the United States makes foreign commitments.[14] In the aftermath of the jar given executive-legislative relations by the Supreme Court decision curbing legislative vetoes (June 23, 1983), the hour is right for a congressional self-examination of how best to supervise the executive branch in foreign affairs. An appropriate starting place would be to modernize the agreement-making process. The agenda for a special inquiry into this subject would include the above recommendations and those suggested in other publications,[15] as well as an examination of the prospects for making the language of statutory agreements more precise, the merits of reconsidering a legislative role in agreement terminations, and the proper degree of involvement (if any) by representatives and their staffs in actual agreement negotiations, in the company of executive diplomats, to mention only a few possibilities.

The suggestions above are modest, workable proposals that could lead to a much more genuine and workable foreign policy partnership between the executive and legislative branches. Ultimately, though, success will depend upon the attitudes of those involved. "The Congress won't be bypassed, and we will be conversant with what goes on," Carl Vinson (D, Georgia,

The Democratic Control of International Agreements

1914–1965), Chairman of the House Armed Services Committee, warned Secretary of Defense Louis Johnson in 1949.[16] Wanting to be conversant—motivation—is the first step toward acquiring the tools to become so. The jury is still out on the question of how intently the Congress really wants the foreign policy partnership its members occasionally promote.

Notes

1. Warren Christopher, "Ceasefire Between the Branches: A Compact in Foreign Affairs," *Foreign Affairs* 60 (Summer 1982), p. 999.
2. "The Making of Treaties and Executive Agreements," *Department of State Bulletin*, 28 April 20, 1953, p. 595.
3. "U.S. Trade Policy: The New Political Dimensions," *Foreign Affairs* 52 (April 1974), p. 477.
4. See *Congressional Record*, 94th Cong., 1st Sess., November 14, 1975, p. 36719.
5. Dated September 1, 1975. See the agreements with Egypt and Israel in *United States and Other International Agreements*, Volume 26, Part 2 (Washington, D.C.: Government Printing Office, 1976), pp. 2271 and 2278 for this passage in both pacts.
6. See P.L. 94-110 and *Congressional Quarterly Almanac 1975* (Washington, D.C.: Congressional Quarterly, Inc., 1976), pp. 344–345.
7. *Congressional Record*, 83 Cong., 2nd Sess., p. 821.
8. Briefing on the Middle East, Committee on Foreign Relations, U.S. Senate., 95th Cong., 1st Sess., February 11, 1977, in the presence of the author (a Committee aide at the time).
9. Interview, Robert L. Chartrand, Senior Specialist in Information Policy and Technology, Congressional Research Service, Library of Congress, Washington, D.C., June 14, 1983. See Robert L. Chartrand and Nancy R. Miller, "The Legislator as User of Information Technology," Report No. 82-185, Congressional Research Service, Library of Congress, November 18, 1982.
10. Stephen E. Frantzich, "Computerized Information Technology in the U.S. House of Representatives," *Legislative Studies Quarterly* 4 (May 1979), p. 268. See also Stephen E. Frantzich, *Computers in Congress: The Politics of Information* (Beverly Hills, Ca.: Sage, 1982).
11. See Linda Schulte, "A Survey of Computerized Legislative Information Systems," *Law Library Journal* 72 (Winter 1979), p. 99.
12. For an indication that at least some Department of State officials have viewed the difference between an executive agreement and a statutory agree-

ment as merely a matter of semantics, see Dean Acheson, *Present at the Creation: My Years in the State Department* (New York: Norton, 1969), p. 72.

13. David J. Kuchenbecker, "Agency-Level Agreements: A New Era in U.S. Treaty Procedure," *Columbia Journal of Transnational Law* 18, 1979, p. 77.

14. Michael J. Glennon, "The Senate Role in Treaty Ratification," *The American Journal of International Law* 77 (April 1983), pp. 257–280.

15. See Glennon, "The Senate Role in Treaty Ratification," and Kuchenbecker, "Agency-Level Agreements."

16. Vance Packard, "Uncle Carl, Watchdog of Defense," *American Magazine* 149 (April 1950), p. 123.

Appendix A
A Sample International Agreement: Liberia, 1969

LIBERIA

Military Mission

The American Ambassador to the Secretary of State of Liberia

EMBASSY OF THE
UNITED STATES OF AMERICA

No. 118   *Monrovia, June 2, 1969*

I have the honor to acknowledge receipt of Your Excellency's Note 11172/DF of May 28, 1969 referring to the Agreement for the Assignment of a United States Military Mission to Liberia signed at Washington on August 7 and October 23, 1953, and

SOURCE: *United States Treaties and Other International Agreements* 20, Part I, 1969 (Washington, D.C.: U.S. Government Printing Office, 1970), pp. 771–772.

Appendix A

on November 18 and December 2, 1957; as amended by Notes exchanged at Monrovia on March 27 and 31, 1959; as extended by Notes exchanged at Monrovia on April 19 and 24, 1961; and as extended and amended by Notes exchanged at Monrovia on December 17, 1963 and April 24, 1964, and advising me of your Government's proposal for the renewal of that Agreement effective as of January 11, 1969 for an additional term of six years.

I have pleasure in advising Your Excellency of my Government's acceptance of this proposal to extend the Agreement for an additional period of six years and its concurrence that this exchange of Notes shall constitute a renewal of the aforementioned Agreement as amended and extended.

Accept, Excellency, the renewed assurances of my highest consideration.

BEN H. BROWN, Jr.

His Excellency
J. RUDOLPH GRIMES,
Secretary of State,
Republic of Liberia.

Appendix B
Regional Classification of America's Agreement Partners

Latin America	Western Europe	Eastern Europe
Argentina	Austria	Bulgaria
Barbados	Belgium	Czechoslovakia
Bolivia	Canada	Poland
Brazil	Cyprus	Romania
Chile	Denmark	Soviet Union
Colombia	Finland	Yugoslavia
Costa Rica	France	
Cuba	Greece	
Dominican Republic	Iceland	
Ecuador	Ireland	
El Salvador	Italy	
Guatemala	Liechtenstein	
Guyana	Luxembourg	
Haiti	Malta	
Honduras	Monaco	
Jamaica	Netherlands	

Appendix B

Mexico	Norway	
Nicaragua	Portugal	
Panama	Spain	
Paraguay	Sweden	
Peru	Switzerland	
Trinidad and Tobago	Turkey	
Uruguay	Vatican	
Venezuela	United Kingdom	
	West Germany	

Africa	*Middle East*	*Asia*
Benin	Afghanistan	Australia
Botswana	Algeria	Burma
Burundi	Bahrein	China, People's Republic of
Cameroon	Egypt	
Chad	Iran	China, Republic of
Central African Republic	Iraq	Fiji
	Israel	India
Congo	Jordan	Indonesia
Ethiopia	Kuwait	Japan
The Gambia	Lebanon	Kampuchea
Gabon	Libya	Laos
Ghana	Morocco	Malaysia
Guinea	Muscat and Oman	Nepal
Ivory Coast	North Yemen	New Zealand
Kenya	Sudan	North Korea
Lesotho	Saudi Arabia	Pakistan
Liberia	Syria	Philippines
Malagasy	Tunisia	Singapore
Mali		Sri Lanka
Malawi		South Korea
Mauritania		South Vietnam
Mauritius		Thailand

Appendix B

Niger
Nigeria
Ruwanda
Senegal
Sierra Leone
Somalia
South Africa
Swaziland
Tanzania
Togo
Uganda
Upper Volta
Zaire
Zambia

Appendix C
Text of the Treaty Powers Resolution

"S. Res. 486

"*Resolved*, That this resolution may be cited as the 'Treaty Powers Resolution'.

"PURPOSE FINDINGS, AND DECLARATION

"Sec. 2. (a) It is the purpose of this resolution to fulfill the intent of the framers of the Constitution and to ensure, through use of the legislative power of the Senate, that no international agreement constituting a treaty will be implemented by the Senate without is prior advice and consent to ratification of that agreement.

"(b) The Senate finds that—

"(1) article I, section 5, clause 2 of the Constitution empowers each House of the Congress to 'dates the Rules of its Proceedings';

SOURCE: "Treaty Powers Resolution," *Hearings*, Senate Foreign Relations Committee, 94th Cong., 2nd Sess., July 21 and 28, 1976, pp. 3–6.

Appendix C

"(2) article II, section 2, clause 2 of the Constitution, empowers the President 'by and with the advice and consent of the Senate to make treaties, provided two-thirds of the Senators present concur';

"(3) the requirement for Senate advice and consent to treaties has in recent years been circumvented by the use of 'executive agreements'; and

"(4) the Senate may, for its part, refuse to authorize and appropriate funds to implement those international agreements which, in its opinion, constitute treaties and to which the Senate has not given its advice and consent to ratification.

"(c) It is the sense of the Senate that, under article 2, section 2, clause 2 of the Constitution, any international agreement, which involves a significant political, military, or economic commitment to a foreign country constitutes a treaty and should be submitted to the Senate for its advice and consent.

"ADVICE

"SEC. 3. It is the sense of the Senate that, in determining whether an international agreement constitutes a treaty under section 2(c) of this resolution, the President should, prior to and during the negotiation of such agreement, seek the advice of the Committee on Foreign Relations.

"CONSENT

"SEC. 4. (a) (1) Where the Senate may, by resolution, express its sense and that any international agreement hereafter entered into which has not been submitted to the Senate for its advice and consent constitutes a treaty under section 2(c) of this resolution and should be so submitted.

"(2) Any such resolution shall be privileged in the same manner and to the same extent as a concurrent resolution of the type described in section 5(c) of the War Powers Resolution is privileged under section 7 (a) and (b) of that law.

"(b) (1) It shall not be in order to consider any bill or joint

Appendix C

resolution or any amendment thereto, or any report of a committee of conference, which authorizes or provides budget authority to implement any international agreement if the Senate has expressed its sense, pursuant to subsection (a) of this section that such agreement constitutes a treaty under section 2(c) of this resolution.

"(2) This subsection shall not apply if the Senate has given it advice and consent to ratification of such agreement.

"(c) Any (1) committee of the Senate which reports any bill or joint resolution, and (2) committee of conference which submits any conference report to the Senate, authorizing or providing budget authority to implement any such agreement, shall so indicate in the committee report or joint statement filed therewith, as the case may be, that such budget authority is authorized or provided in such bill, resolution, or conference report."

Appendix D
The Sparkman-Bennet Letters of 1978

U.S. SENATE,
COMMITTEE OF FOREIGN RELATIONS,
July 28, 1978.

HON. DOUGLAS J. BENNET, Jr.,
Assistant Secretary for Congressional Relations, Department of State, Washington, D.C.

DEAR MR. BENNET: Thank you for your recent letter proposing a consultative procedure to be followed in the case of significant international agreements to be entered into by the United States.

I am pleased to accept your proposal to inform the committee periodically on a confidential basis, of significant international agreements which have been authorized for negotiation pursuant to the Circular 175 procedure. I would hope that, notwithstanding this reference to the Circular 175 procedure,

SOURCE: "International Agreements Consultation Resolution," Senate Report No. 95-1171, 95th Cong., 2nd Sess., August 25, 1978, pp. 203.

Appendix D

consultation would take place with respect to agreements to be negotiated not only by the Department of State but by other departments and agencies as well. I believe that, to be meaningful, a consultative mechanism must cover all significant internatiional agreements contemplated by the United States, regardless of the executive entity involved in the negotiation or approval processes.

I would hope, in addition, that the committee would be consulted on the question of whether a certain arrangement will be regarded as an international agreement, as it was in the case of the unilateral policy declaration regarding continued adherence to the terms of the SALT I agreement. This is, as you know, a subject on which the committee has taken an increased interest in recent years, and I believe consultations on this question can be productive for both branches.

I appreciate your cooperation, and you may be assured that the committee will make every effort to make this procedure work.

Best wishes,
Sincerely,

JOHN SPARKMAN, *Chairman.*

DEPARTMENT OF STATE,
Washington, D.C.

Hon. JOHN J. SPARKMAN,
Chairman, Committee on Foreign Relations,
U.S. Senate.

DEAR MR. CHAIRMAN: The Department would like to work out a more systematic method of consulting with you and your committee on the form of significant U.S. international agreements.

Appendix D

If agreeable to you, we propose to send you periodically a confidential list of significant international agreements which have been authorized for negotiation pursuant to the Circular 175 procedure. The list would briefly describe the subject matter of the agreements listed and indicate their anticipated form.

I suggest that the committee in turn advise the Department of any listed agreement as to which it desires to consult concerning its form.

Then we would proceed with the actual consultation.

I hope that this suggestion meets with your approval. If it does, we are prepared to start immediately.

Sincerely,

DOUGLAS J. BENNET, Jr.,
Assistant Secretary for Congressional Relations.

Bibliography

Ackerman, Lee B. "Executive Agreements, the Treatymaking Clause, and Strict Constructionism." *Loyola University of Los Angeles Law Review* 8 (September 1975): 587–631.
Aspin, Les. "The Defense Budget and Foreign Policy: The Role of Congress." *Daedalus* 104 (Summer 1975): 155–174.
———. "Congress versus the Defense Department." In *The Tethered Presidency*, edited by Thomas M. Franck. New York: New York University Press, 1981.
Atwood, Brian J. "Downtown Perspective: Lessons on Liaison with Congress." In *The Tethered Presidency*, edited by Thomas M. Franck. New York: New York University Press, 1981.
Baldwin, Gordon B. "Congressional Power to Demand Disclosure of Foreign Intelligence Agreements," *Brooklyn Journal of International Law* 3 (1976): 1–30.
Barber, Hollis W. *Foreign Policies of the United States*. New York: Dryden, 1953.
Barnett, J. T. "International Agreements Without the Advice and Consent of the Senate." *Yale Law Journal* 15 (1905): 18–27.
Bemis, Samuel F. *A Diplomatic History of the United States*. 5th ed. New York: Holt, Rinehart and Winston, 1965.
Bennet, Douglas J. "Congress and Foreign Policy: Who Needs It?" 57 *Foreign Affairs* (Fall 1978): 40–50.
———. "Congress: Its Role in Foreign Policymaking." *Department of State Bulletin* 78 (June 1978): 35–36.

Bibliography

Berger, Raoul. "President's Unilateral Termination of the Taiwan Treaty." *Northwestern University Law Review* 75 (1980): 577–634.
———. "The Presidential Monopoly of Foreign Relations." *Michigan Law Review* 71 (1972): 1–59.
Bestor, Arthur. "Respective Roles of Senate and President in the Making and Abrogation of Treaties—The Original Intent of the Framers of the Constitution Historically Examined." *Washington Law Review* 55 (1979): 1–135.
Borchard, Edwin M. "Treaties and Executive Agreements." *American Political Science Review* 40 (1946): 731–32.
———. "Treaties and Executive Agreements—A Reply." *Yale Law Journal* 54 (1945): 616–659.
"Bricker and the UN." *New Republic* 132 (May 2, 1955): 5.
Bridge, Robert L. "The New Air Force International Agreement Procedures." *The Reporter* (Office of the Judge Advocate General of the Air Force) 5 (August 1978): 10–22.
Brown, Ben H., Jr. "Congress and the Department of State." *Annals of the American Academy of Political and Social Science* 289 (September 1953): 100–107.
Browne, Marjorie Ann. "Executive Agreements and the Congress." Congressional Research Service, Issue Brief No. 1B75035, February 27, 1981.
Butler, Charles Henry. *The Treaty Making Power of the United States.* New York: Banks Law Book, 1902.
Byrd, Elbert M., Jr. *Treaties and Executive Agreements in the United States: Their Separate Roles and Limitations.* The Hague: Martinus Nijhoff, 1960.
Call, Joseph L. "Government by Decree Through Executive Agreement," *Baylor Law Review* 6 (1954): 277.
Carney, Francis M. "Ideological Groups in the U.S. Senate, 1953–1958, as Indicated by Scale Analysis." unpublished paper, University of California, Riverside, 1960.
Case, Clifford. "Statement in Support of Amendment on International Agreements." *Congressional Record.* Daily ed., v. 122, June 11, 1976: S9031–S9033.
———. "Study on Tardy Executive Agreements." *Congressional Record.* Daily ed., v. 123, May 23, 1977: S8353–S8354.
Casper, Gerhard. "Constitutional Constraints on the Conduct of Foreign and Defense Policy: A Nonjudicial Model." *University of Chicago Review* 43 (Spring 1976): 463–98.

Bibliography

Cassidy, Robert C., Jr. "Negotiating About Negotiations: The Geneva Multilateral Trade Talks." In *The Tethered Presidency*, edited by Thomas M. Franck. New York: New York University Press, 1981.

Catudal, H. M. "Executive Agreements: A Supplement to the Treaty-Making Procedure." *George Washington Law Review* 10 (1941-1942): 653-669.

Christopher, Warren. "Ceasefire Between the Branches: A Compact in Foreign Affairs." *Foreign Affairs* 60 (Summer 1982): 989-1005.

Church, Frank. "Of Presidents and Caesars: The Decline of Constitutional Government in the Conduct of American Foreign Policy," *Idaho Law Review* 6 (Fall 1969): 1-15. Revised and reprinted in *Congressional Record*, 91st Cong., 2d Sess., April 30, 1970: 13563-13566.

———. "Carter on the Sinking of SALT: That's Not the Way I Remember It," *Washington Post*, November 19, 1982.

Cohen, Morris L. "U.S. Treaties." in his *Legal Research in a Nutshell*. St. Paul, Minn.: West Publishing, 1978.

Cohen, Richard. "Self-Executing Executive Agreements." *Buffalo Law Review* 24 (1974): 137-158.

Collins, Laurence. "Treaties and/or Statutes." *Cambridge Law Journal* 33 (1974): 181-86.

Combs, Jerald A. *The Jay Treaty*. Berkeley: University of California Press, 1970.

Commager, Henry Steele. "The Perilous Folly of Senator Bricker." *The Reporter* 9 (October 13, 1953): 12-17.

Constitutional Amendment Relative to Treaties and Executive Agreements. Senate Reports nos. 412 and 1716, June 15, 1953, and April 11, 1956.

Corwin, Edward S. "The President's Treaty-Making Power." *Think* 19 (July 1953).

———. *The President: Office and Powers, 1787-1948*. 3rd ed. New York: New York University, 1948.

———. *The President's Control of Foreign Relations*. Princeton: Princeton University Press, 1917.

———. *National Supremacy: Treaty Power versus State Power*. New York: Holt, 1913.

Crabb, Cecil V. Jr., and Pat Holt. *Invitation to Struggle: Congress, the President and Foreign Policy*. Washington, D.C.: Congressional Quarterly, 1980.

Bibliography

Dahl, Robert A. *Congress and Foreign Policy.* New York: Harcourt, Brace, 1950.

Dean, Arthur H. "The Bricker Amendment and Authority Over Foreign Affairs." *Foreign Affairs* 32 (October 1953): 1–19.

Destler, I. M. "Treaty Troubles: Versailles in Reverse." *Foreign Policy* 33 (Winter 1978–79): 45–65.

———. "Trade Consensus, SALT Stalemate: Congress and Foreign Policy in the 1970s." In *The New Congress*, edited by Thomas E. Mann and Norman J. Ornstein. Washington, D.C.: American Enterprise Institute, 1981.

———. "Dateline Washington: Congress as Boss?" *Foreign Policy* 42 (Spring 1981): 167–80.

———. "Dateline Washington: Life After The Veto," *Foreign Policy*, 52 (Fall 1983): 181–86.

Donovan, Robert J. *Eisenhower: The Inside Story.* New York: Harper, 1956.

Dulles, John Foster. "The Making of Treaties and Executive Agreements." *Department of State Bulletin* 28 (April 20, 1953): 591–595.

———. "United States Constitution and United Nations Charter: An Appraisal." *Department of State Bulletin* 29 (September 7, 1953): 307–310.

Eisenhower, Dwight D. *The White House Years: Mandate for Change, 1953–1956.* New York: Doubleday, 1963.

Emerson, J. Terry. "The Legislative Role in Treaty Abrogation." *Journal of Legislation* 5 (1978): 46–80.

"Exclusive Interview with Senator Bricker." *Newsweek* 45 (January 10, 1955): 20.

"Executive Agreements: A Survey of Recent Congressional Interest and Action." *Supplementary Reports on Intelligence Activities*, Final Report (Book VI), Select Committee on Intelligence (the Church Committee), U.S. Senate, 94th Congress, 2d Session. Report No. 94-755, 1976: 355–364.

Finch, George A. "The Need to Restrain the Treaty-Making Powers of the United States Within Constitutional Limits." *American Journal of International Law* 48 (1954): 57–82.

Fisher, Louis. *The Constitution Between Friends: Congress, the President, and the Law.* New York: St. Martin's, 1978.

———. *The President and Congress: Power and Policy.* New York: Free Press, 1972.

Fitzgerald, Peter L. "Executive Agreements and the Intent Behind

Bibliography

the Treaty Power." *Hastings Constitutional Law Quarterly*, v. 2 no. 3 (Summer 1975): 757–771.

Fleming, D. F. "Role of the Senate in Treaty Making." *American Political Science Review* 583 (1934): 583–598.

Franck, Thomas M. "Word Made Law: The Decision of the ICS in the Nuclear Test Cases." *American Journal of International Law* 69 (1975): 612–623.

———, and Edward Weisband. *Foreign Policy by Congress*. New York: Oxford, 1979.

———. "Advice and Consent." *New York Times*, February 28, 1978.

———. "Congress As A World Power." *Worldview* 22 (October 1979): 4–7.

Fulbright, J. William. *The Crippled Giant*. New York: Random House, 1972.

———. "In Thrall to Fear." *The New Yorker* 47, January 8, 1971, pp. 41–62.

Garner, James W. "Acts and Joint Resolutions of Congress as Substitutes for Treaties." *American Journal of International Law* 29 (1935): 482–487.

Garrett, Stephen A. "Foreign Policy and the American Constitution: The Bricker Amendment in Contemporary Perspective." *International Studies Quarterly* 16 (June 1972): 187–220.

Gelb, Leslie H. "A Domestic Challenge to Executive Agreements." *New York Times*, August 17, 1975.

Gilbert, Amy M. *Executive Agreements and Treaties, 1946–1973*. New York: Thomas-Newell, 1973.

Glennon, Michael J. "Remarks on the Panel on Treaties and Executive Agreements." Annual meeting, American Society of International Law, San Francisco, April 23, 1977. Mimeographed.

———. "Treaty Process Reform: Saving Constitutionalism Without Destroying Diplomacy." *University of Cincinnati Law Review* 512 (1983): 84–107.

———. "The Senate Role in Treaty Ratification." *American Journal of International Law* 2 (April 1983): 257–80.

Goldwater, Barry. "President's Constitutional Primacy in Foreign Relations and National Defense." *Virginia Journal of International Law* 463 (1973).

Hamilton, Alexander. "Federalist Paper No. 75." In *Federalist Papers*. New York: Modern Library, 1937.

Hamilton, Lee H., and Michael H. Van Dusen. "Making the Sepa-

ration of Powers Work." *Foreign Affairs* 57 (Fall 1978): 17–39.
Henkin, Louis. *Foreign Affairs and the Constitution.* Mineola, New York: Foundation Press, 1972.
———. " 'A More Effective System' for Foreign Relations: The Constitutional Framework." In "Symposium—Organizing the Government to Conduct Foreign Policy: The Constitutional Questions." *Virginia Law Review* 61 (1975): 747–755.
———. "The Treaty Makers and the Law Makers: The Law of the Land and Foreign Relations." *University of Pennsylvania Law Review* 107 (1959): 903–936.
Herter, Christian A. "Relation of the House of Representatives to the Making and Implementation of Treaties." *Proceedings of the American Society of International Law* 45 (1951): 55–60.
Hopson, Everett G. "The Executive Agreement in United States Practice." *Air Force JAG Law Review* (Fall 1970).
Hughes, Emmet John. *The Ordeal of Power.* New York: Atheneum, 1962.
Humphrey, Hubert H. "The Senate in Foreign Policy," *Foreign Affairs* 37 (July 1959): 525–536.
"International Agreements: An Analysis of Executive Regulations and Practices." Congressional Research Service, Library of Congress, 95th Congress, 1st Session (1977).
Johnson, Loch. "Legislators as Diplomats: The Czechoslovak Gold Dispute." *Journal of Legislation* 9 (Winter 1982): 36–51.
———. "The U.S. Congress and the CIA: Monitoring the Dark Side of Government." *Legislative Studies Quarterly* 4 (November 1980).
———. "The CIA: Controlling the Quiet Option." *Foreign Policy* 39 (Summer 1980): 143–153.
———, and James M. McCormick. "Foreign Policy by Executive Fiat." *Foreign Policy* 28 (Fall 1977): 117–138.
———. "The Making of International Agreements: A Reappraisal of Congressional Involvement." *Journal of Politics* 40 (May 1978): 468–478.
———. "The Democratic Control of International Commitments." *Presidential Studies Quarterly* 8 (Summer 1978): 275–283.
Kaiser, Fred. "Oversight of Foreign Policy: The U.S.. House Committee on International Relations." *Legislative Studies Quarterly* 2 (August 1977).
Kirkpatrick, Jeane J. "Dictatorships and Double Standards." *Commentary* 68 (November 1979): 34–45.

Bibliography

Kissinger, Henry. *Years of Upheaval*. Boston: Little, Brown, 1982.
———. *White House Years*. Boston: Little, Brown, 1979.
———. *A World Restored*. New York: Houghton Mifflin, 1957.
"Knights and Knaves in Eisenhower's Great Crusade." *New Republic* 127, (July 28, 1952): 14.
Koenig, Louis W. *The Chief Executive*. New York: Harcourt, Brace & World, 1964.
Kuchenbecker, David J. "Agency-Level Executive Agreements: A New Era in U.S. Treaty Practice." *Columbia Journal of Transnational Law*, 18 (1979): 1–77.
Lawson, Karin L. "The Constitutional Twilight Zone of Treaty Termination: *Goldwater v. Carter*." *Virginia Journal of International Law* 20 (Fall 1979): 147–69.
Leary, Margaret A. "International Executive Agreements: A Guide to Legal Issues and Research Sources." *Law Library Journal* 72 (1979): 1–11.
Leigh, Monroe. "The Congress, the President and Executive Agreements." In *Proceedings and Committee Reports of the American Branch of the International Law Association: 1975–1976*. New York: American Branch ILA, 1976.
Levitan, D. M. "Executive Agreements: A Study of the Executive in the Control of the Foreign Relations of the United States." *Illinois Law Review* 35 (1940).
Lowi, Theodore J. "Bases in Spain." In *American Civil-Military Decisions*, edited by Harold Stein. Birmingham: University of Alabama, 1963.
McClure, Wallace M. *International Executive Agreements: Democratic Procedure under the Constitution of the United States*. New York: Columbia University Press, 1941.
McDougal, Myres S. and Asher Lans. "Treaties and Congressional-Executive or Presidential Agreements: Interchangeable Instruments of National Policy." *Yale Law Journal* 54 (March 1945): 181–351, and (June 1945): 534–615.
McLaughlin, C. H. "Scope of the Treaty Power in the United States." *Minnesota Law Review* 43 (1959).
Majak, R. Roger. *International Agreements: An Analysis of Executive Regulations and Practices*. Washington, D.C.: Congressional Research Service, Library of Congress, September 1976.
Manning, Bayless. "The Congress, the Executive Affairs: Three Proposals." *Foreign Affairs* 55 (January 1977).

Bibliography

Marchetti, Victor, and John D. Marks. *The CIA and the Cult of Intelligence.* New York: Knopf, 1974.

Marks, Lee R. "Legislating and the Conduct of Diplomacy: The Constitution's Inconsistent Functions." In *The Tethered Presidency,* edited by Thomas M. Franck. New York: New York University Press, 1981.

Mathews, Craig. "The Constitutional Power of the President to Conclude International Agreements." *The Yale Law Journal* 63 (January 1955): 345–389.

Merin, Kenneth D. "The Treaty Power and Congressional Power in Conflict." *Seton Hall Law Review* 8 (1977).

Meron, Theodor. "The Treaty Power: The International Legal Effect of Changes in Obligations Initiated by the Congress." In *The Tethered Presidency,* edited by Thomas M. Franck. New York: New York University Press, 1981.

Moe, Richard C., and Steven C. Teel. "Congress as Policy Maker: A Necessary Reappraisal." In *The Politics of U.S. Foreign Policy Making,* edited by Douglas M. Fox. Pacific Palisades, California: Goodyear, 1971.

Moore, John Bassett. "Treaties and Executive Agreements." *Political Science Quarterly* 20 (1905): 385–390.

Morley, Felix. *Treaty Law and the Constitution.* New York: American Enterprise Institute, 1953.

Murphy, John F. "Treaties and International Agreements Other Than Treaties: Constitutional Allocation of Power and Responsibility Among the President, the House of Representatives, and the Senate." *University of Kansas Law Review* v. 23, no. 2 (Winter 1975): 221–248.

Nelson, Randall H. "Legislative Participation in the Treaty and Agreement Making Process." *Western Political Quarterly* 13 (March 1961): 154–171.

"New Bricker Amendment." *U.S. News & World Report* 40 (March 23, 1956): 16.

Newhouse, John. *Cold Dawn: The Story of SALT.* New York: Holt, Rinehart, and Winston, 1973.

Newman, Frank C. and Keaton, Harry J. "Congress and the Faithful Execution of Laws—Should Legislators Supervise Administrators?" *California Law Review* 41 (Winter 1953–54): 565–95.

Ohly, D. Christopher. "Advice and Consent: International Executive

Bibliography

Claims Settlement Agreements." *California Western International Law Journal* v. 5, no. 2 (Spring 1975): 271–296.
Paige, Joseph. *The Law Nobody Knows*. New York: Vantage, 1977.
Pastor, Robert A. *Congress and the Politics of US Foreign Economic Policy 1929–1976*. Berkeley: University of California Press, 1980.
Percy, Charles H. "The Partisan Gap." *Foreign Policy* 45 (Winter 1981/82): 3–15.
Perkins, Dexter. *The Monroe Doctrine*. Cambridge, Mass.: Harvard University Press, 1932.
Price, Hugh P. *The Bricker Amendment*. The Legislative Reference Service: JX 235 A, December 2, 1964.
Pusey, Merlo J. "Bricker Amendment." *The Nation* 176 (February 14, 1953): 280–282.
Rehm, John B. "Making Foreign Policy Through International Agreement." In *The Constitution and the Conduct of Foreign Policy*, edited by Francis O. Wilcox and Richard A. Frank. New York: Praeger, 1976.
Riggs, John H., Jr. "Termination of Treaties by the Executive Without Congressional Approval: The Case of the Warsaw Convention." *Journal of Air Law and Commerce* 32 (1966): 526–534.
Robinson, James A. *Congress and Foreign Policy-Making: A Study in Legislative Influence and Initiative*. Homewood, Illinois: Dorsey, 1962.
Rogers Lindsay. "Senator Bricker Finds a Loophole." *The Reporter* 7 (July 22, 1952): 31–33.
Rosenau, James N. "The Nomination of 'Chip' Bohlen." Eagleton Institute Case Study No. 1. New York: McGraw-Hill, 1960.
Rositzke, Harry. *CIA's Secret Operations: Espionage, Counter Espionage, and Covert Action*. New York: Reader's Digest, 1977.
Rovine, Arthur W. "Separation of Powers and International Executive Agreements." *Indiana Law Journal* 52 (1977): 397–431.
———. *Digest of U.S. Practice of International Law*. Washington, D.C.: Government Printing Office, 1974.
Sale, David M. *Executive Agreements: A Survey of Legal and Political Controversies Concerning Their Use in United States Practice*. JX 235A. Washington, D.C.: Congressional Research Service, Library of Congress, February 13, 1975.
Sato, I. "Treaties and the Constitution." *Washington Law Review* 43 (1938).

Bibliography

Scheffer, David J. "The Law of Treaty Termination as Applied to the U.S. Re-Recognition of the Republic of China." *Harvard International Law Journal* 19 (Fall 1978): 931–1009.

Schlesinger, Arthur, Jr. *The Imperial Presidency.* New York: Houghton Mifflin, 1973.

——. "Congress and the Making of American Foreign Policy." *Foreign Affairs* 51 (October 1972): 78–113.

Schmitt, Gary James. *Executive Agreements and Separation of Powers: Military Agreements from 1946–1976.* Ph.D. dissertation, University of Chicago, 1980.

Schollaert, James T. "A Critique of Recent U.S. Practice of International Agreements Law." Annual meeting, American Society of International Law, San Francisco, April 23, 1977. Mimeographed.

Schubert, Glendon A. "Politics and the Constitution: The Bricker Amendment During 1953." *Journal of Politics* 16 (May 1954): 257–298.

Slonim, Solomon. "Congressional-Executive Agreements." *Columbia Journal of Transnational Law* 14 (1975): 434–50.

Smith, Gerard C. *Doubletalk: The Story of the First Strategic Arms Limitations Talks* Garden City, N.Y.: Doubleday, 1980.

Snyder, Richard C., and Edgar S. Furniss, Jr. *American Foreign Policy.* New York: Rinehard, 1954.

Sparkman, John. "Certain Middle East Agreements." *Congressional Record.* Daily ed. V. 122, Feb. 17, 1976: S1687–S1692.

——. "The President's Power to Enter into International Agreements." *Congressional Record.* Daily ed. V. 121, Nov. 14, 1975: S20102–S20115.

——. "Checks and Balances in American Foreign Policy." *Indiana Law Journal* 52 (1977): 433–447.

Stebbins, Richard P. *The United States in World Affairs, 1953;* New York: Harper, 1955.

——. *The United States in World Affairs, 1954.* New York: Harper, 1956.

Stennis, John, and J. William Fulbright. *The Role of Congress in Foreign Policy.* Washington, D.C.: American Enterprise Institute, 1971.

Stevens, Charles J. "The Use and Control of Executive Agreements: Recent Congressional Initiatives." *Orbis* 20 (Winter 1977): 905–931.

Stevenson, John R. "Constitutional Aspects of the Executive Agree-

Bibliography

ment Procedure." *Department of State Bulletin* 66 (June 19, 1972): 840–51.

Sutherland, Arthur. "The Bricker Amendment, Executive Agreements and Imported Potatoes." *Harvard Law Review* 65 (June 1952): 1305–38.

———. "Restricting the Treaty Power." *Harvard Law Review* 65 (1952): 1305.

———. "The Flag, the Constitituion, and International Agreements." *Harvard Law Review* 68 (1955).

Tansill, Charles C. "The Treaty-Making Powers of the Senate." *American Journal of International Law* 459 (1924): 462–70.

Taylor, Stan A. "Congressional Resurgence," In *Problems of American Foreign Policy*, edited by Martin B. Hickman. 2nd ed. Beverly Hills: Benziger, Bruce, and Glencoe, 1975.

Tomain, Joseph P. "Executive Agreements and the Bypassing of Congress." *Journal of International Law and Economics* 8 (1973): 129–39.

Tower, John G. "Congress Versus the President: The Formulation and Implementation of American Foreign Policy." *Foreign Affairs* (Winter 1981–82): 229–246.

Tucker, Henry St. George. *Limitations on the Treaty-Making Power*. New York: The Ronald Press Company, 1915.

Treaties and Other International Acts Series. Washington, D.C.: Government Printing Office.

U.S. Army. "Authorization and Responsibility for Negotiating, Concluding, Forwarding, and Depositing of International Agreements." Army Regulation No. 550-51 (15 June 1978).

U.S. Congress. House. Committee on Foreign Affairs. Subcommittee on National Security Policy and Scientific Developments. "International Executive Agreements." Hearing, 92d Congress, 2d session, on S. 596, H.R. 14365, and H.R. 14647. June 19, 1972. Washington, D.C.: U.S. Government Printing Office, 1972.

———. House. Committee on Foreign Affairs. "Transmittal of Executive Agreements to Congress." 92d Congress, 2d session. House. Report No. 92-1301. Report to accompany S. 596, Aug. 3, 1972. Washington, D.C.: U.S. Government Printing Office, 1972.

———. House. Committee on International Relations. Subcommittee on International Security and Scientific Affairs. "Congressional Review of International Agreements." Hearings, 94th Congress, 2d

Bibliography

session. June 22, 23, 29, and 30, July 20 and 22, 1976. Washington, D.C.: U.S. Government Printing Office, 1976.

U.S. Congress. Senate. Committee on Government Operations, "U.S. Participation in International Organizations." 95th Cong., 1st Sess. (1977). Report No. 95-50.

———. Senate. Committee on Foreign Relations. "Agreements between the United States and Spain." 91st Congress, 2d Session. Senate. Report No. 91-1425. Report to accompany S. Res. 469. Washington, D.C.: U.S. Government Printing Office, 1970.

———. "U.S. Security Agreements and Commitments Abroad." *Hearings*, October 1969.

———. "U.S. Commitments to Foreign Powers." *Hearings*, August and September, 1967.

———. "Spanish Base Agreement." *Hearing*, 91st Congress, 2d Session, on S. Res. 469. Aug. 26, 1970. Washington, D.C.: U.S. Government Printing Office, 1970.

———. "Transmittal of Executive Agreements to Congress," *Hearings*, 92d Congress. 1st Session, on S. 596. Oct. 20 and 21, 1971. Washington, D.C.: U.S. Government Printing Office, 1971.

———. "Executive Agreements with Portugal and Bahrain." *Hearings*, 92d Congress, 2d session, on S. Res. 214. Feb. 1, 2, and 3, 1972. Washington D.C.: U.S. Government Printing Office, 1972.

———. "Agreements with Portugal and Bahrain." 92d Congress, 2d session. Senate. Report No. 92-632. Report to accompany S. Res. 214. Feb. 17, 1972. Washington D.C.: U.S. Government Printing Office, 1972.

———. "Warning System in Sinai." *Hearings*. 94th Congress, 1st Session, October 6 and 7, 1975. Washington, D.C.: U.S. Government Printing Office, 1976.

———. "Treaty Powers Resolution." *Hearings*. 94th Congress, 2d Session, on S. Res. 486, July 21 and 28, 1976. Washington, D.C.: U.S. Government Printing Office, 1976.

———. Senate. Committee on the Judiciary. "Treaties and Executive Agreements." *Hearings*. 82d Congress, 2d Session on S.J. Res. 130. May 1952. Washington, D.C.: U.S. Government Printing Office, 1952.

———. Senate. Committee on Armed Services. "Worldwide Military Commitments." *Hearings*. August 25 and 30, 1966.

———. Subcommittee on Separation of Powers. "Congressional Over-

Bibliography

sight of Executive Agreements." *Hearings.* 92d Congress, 2d Session on S. 3475. Apr. 24 and 25, May 12, 18, 19, 1972. Washington, D.C.: U.S. Government Printing Office, 1972.

———. Senate. "Treaties and Executive Agreements." *Hearings.* 83d Congress, 1st session on S.J. Res. 1 and S.J. Res. 43. Feb. 1953, Washington, D.C.

———. "Treaties and Executive Agreements." *Hearings.* 84th Congress, 1st session on S.J. Res. 1. Apr. 1955. Washington, D.C.: U.S. Government Printing Office, 1955.

———. "Treaties and Executive Agreements." *Hearings.* 85th Congress, 1st session, on S.J. Res. 3. June 25, 1957. Washington, D.C.: U.S. Government Printing Office, 1958.

———. "Congressional Oversight of Executive Agreements." 93d Congress, 2d session. Senate. Report No. 93-1286. Report to accompany S. 3830, Nov. 18, 1974. Washington, D.C.: U.S. Government Printing Office, 1974.

———. "Congressional Oversight of Executive Agreements—1975." *Hearings.* 94th Congress, 1st Session on S. 632 and S. 1251: May 13, 14, 15, July 25, 1975. Washington, D.C.: U.S. Government Printing Office, 1976.

U.S. Department of State. Office of the Legal Adviser for Treaty Affairs. "International Agreements Other than Treaties, 1946–1968: A List with Citation of Their Legal Basis." January 10, 1969 supplemented with an addendum through 1974. Mimeographed.

U.S. General Accounting Office. "U.S. Agreements with the Republic of Korea." Report of the Comptroller General of the United States. (ID-76-20; Feb. 20, 1976.) Washington D.C., 1976.

———. "Reporting of U.S. International Agreements by Executive Agencies Has Improved." Report of the Comptroller General of the United States. (ID-78-57; Oct. 31, 1978.) Washington, D.C.: 1978.

U.S. Treaties and Other International Agreements. Washington, D.C.: Government Printing Office.

Weinfeld, Abraham C. "Comment: What Did the Framers of the Federal Constitution Mean by 'Agreements or Compacts.' " *University of Chicago Law Review* 3 (1935–36): 457.

Wertenbaker, William. "A Report at Large: Law of the Sea," *The New Yorker* (August 1, 1983): 38–65.

Whalen, Charles W., Jr. *The House and Foreign Policy.* Chapel Hill: University of North Carolina Press, 1982.

Bibliography

Whitton, John B. and Fowler, J. Edward. "Bricker Amendment—Fallacies and Dangers." *American Journal of International Law*, 48 (1954): 23–56.
"Why a Loyal Republican Wants to Limit Ike's Power." *U.S. News & World Report* 36 (January 29, 1954): 74.
Wilcox, Francis O. *Congress, the Executive, and Foreign Policy.* New York: Harper & Row, 1971.
Wilson, R. R. "International Law of Treaties in the U.S." *American Journal of International Law* 31 (1937).
Wolfers, Arnold. *Discord and Collaboration: Essays on International Politics.* Baltimore: Johns Hopkins University Press, 1962.
Wright, Quincy. "The United States and International Agreements." *American Journal of International Law* 38 (1944): 341–355.
Wriston, H. M. *Executive Agents in American Foreign Relations.* London: Oxford University Press, 1929.
Zwirn, Jerrold. *Congressional Publications: A Research Guide to Legislation, Budgets, and Treaties.* Littleton, Colorado: Libraries Unlimited, 1983.

Index

Acheson, Dean, 90, 175
Africa, 44–48, 75–76, 90, 179–180
Agency for International Development (AID), 68, 129
Agency-to-agency agreements, 128, 130, 173
Albania, 77
Allende, Salvador, 77–78
American Bar Association, 93, 102
American Farm Bureau Federation, 93
American Federation of Labor, 92
American Legion, 93
American Medical Association, 93
American Veterans' Committee, 93
Antigenocide convention, 89, 98
Asia, 44–48, 54, 71, 179
Aspin, Les, 127
Assassination plots, 76–77
Atomic Energy Act (1945), 136, 137
Atomic Energy Commission, 129
Atwood, J. Brian, 66
Audits, 171
Authoritarian regimes, 32–36, 39–41, 50, 53, 80
AWACS (Airborne Warning and Control System), 138
Azores, 57, 60

Bahrain, 57, 61
Baldwin, Gordon B., 152
Banks, Arthur, 32
Barber, Hollis W., 4
Bayh, Birch, 136
Belmont, 110
Bennet, Douglas J., Jr., 145, 171, 184–186
Bentsen, Floyd, 138, 147
Berger, Raoul, 4
Bicameral disputes, 139, 147–150
Biden, Joseph, 136
Bingham, Jonathan B., 137
Bohlen-Serrano Agreement, 67
Brazil, 50, 59
Bricker Amendment, 91–100, 103, 105–106, 109, 111, 114, 116, 145, 146, 152
Bricker, John W., 85–86, 89, 91–92, 102–104, 106, 108, 117, 163
Browne, Marjorie Ann, 112, 129
Brownell, Herbert, 92, 94–95, 97, 100
Buckley, William F., 116
Burchinal, David, 64
Burton, John L., 154
Bush, George, 80

Canada, 50, 60, 87, 154
Caribbean, 59

201

Index

Carney, Francis M., 90
Carter, Jimmy, 52, 74, 129, 130, 140–141, 155, 156
Case Amendment (1973), 140
Case, Clifford, 6, 70–71, 121, 129, 140, 144
Case Substitute (to the Treaty Powers Resolution, 1978), 144–146, 147
Case-Zablocki Act (the Case Act), 121, 122–136, 150, 151, 165–166, 168
  lateness in reporting, 123–125, 129–130
  1977 Amendment to, 124
  increase in reporting under, 128–129
  1978 Amendment to, 130–131
  legislative procedures, 131–132
  computer storage, 165–166, 168, 172
Castro, Fidel, 77
Central Intelligence Agency (CIA), 33, 73–79, 126, 135–136, 151
Chamber of Commerce of the United States, 93
Chartrand, Robert L., 174
Chile, 77–78
China, People's Republic of (PRC), 57, 60, 77
China, Republic of (Taiwan), 50, 142, 156
Christopher, Warren, 160
Church Committee, 77–78, 81–82
Church, Frank, 27, 64, 66, 71, 116, 117–118, 149
Church Resolution (Spain), 66, 120
Circular 175 procedure, 184–186
Claims agreements, 11
Clark, Dick, 59, 140–141, 147, 148; see also, Treaty Powers Resolution
Clifford, Clark, 19
Cold War, 14, 17, 29, 57
Commager, Henry Steele, 95, 97, 100
Commander-in-chief, 57, 61; see also, presidential power
Common Market, 15
Communication agreements, 11–12, 18, 25, 36–39, 51, 100, 126
Communism, 17, 32, 53, 63
Computer-assisted monitoring of international agreements, 132, 164–173; see also, SCORPIO, FLITE
Congress, U.S., 19–20, 26, 43, 56–57, 61, 70, 74, 85–86, 90, 95, 98–99, 106, 118, 122, 126, 138–139, 146–147, 150–151, 158–160, 173
Congressional Research Service, 171–172
Constitution, U.S., 3, 86–89, 92, 94, 98, 100–101, 106, 110, 122, 148–149
Constitutional balance, 118, 120, 122, 133, 135, 141, 159–160, 173
Corwin, Edward S., 93, 95, 98, 99
Covert action (CA) agreements, 74–79, 126, 135; see also, Central Intelligence Agency
"Creeping commitments," 69
Cuba, 77
Cultural-technical agreements, 11–12, 15, 17, 36–39, 51, 126

Daughters of the American Revolution, 93–94
Democratic Party, 104, 114, 145
Democratic regimes, 32–36, 39–41
Destler, I. M., 155
Détente, 53
Diebold, William, Jr., 161
Diego Garcia, 8, 57, 61, 64
Diez-Alegria, Manuel, 64
Diplomatic agreements, 11–12, 15, 18, 23, 25
Dirksen, Everett McKinley, 115
Dominican Republic, 77
Dong, Pham Van, 70
Donovan, Robert J., 50
Douglas, William O., 88
Dulles, Allen, 73, 78
Dulles, John Foster, 29, 64, 67, 92, 99, 100, 109–110, 113, 147, 161
Duvalier, "Papa Doc," 78

Eastern Europe, 44–48, 72, 178
Economic and trade agreements, 10, 15, 25, 36–39, 51, 54, 72, 126
Ecuador, 78
Education agreements, 11–12
Egypt, 72, 161, 174
El Salvador, 60
Eisenhower, Dwight D., 15, 17, 21, 25, 34–35, 45, 59, 61, 66–67, 92, 101–104, 107, 111, 114

Index

Ellender, Allen J., 115
Ervin, Sam J., Jr., 119, 138
Ethiopia, 57, 60, 66
Executive Agreement Index (EAI), 23–25, 59, 61–63
Executive agreements, 5, 7, 8, 9, 12, 19, 23, 24, 25, 40–42, 46–48, 51, 56, 88–91, 98–100, 102, 106, 119, 120, 121, 128, 131–132, 138, 163
  substantive agreements, 58
  administrative agreements, 58
Executive-legislative compact, 160; *see also*, constitutional balance
Executive privilege, 163–164

Ferguson, Homer, 105, 152
Finch, George, 112
Fisher, Louis, 27, 112
Fishery Conservation and Management Act (1976), 137, 155
Flanders, Ralph E., 108
FLITE (federal legal information through electronics), 170–172
Ford, Gerald R., 61, 72, 155, 162
Foreign aid, 120
Forward deployment, 58
France, 50
Frantzich, Stephen E., 164–165
Frye, Alton, 158
Fujii v. California, 89, 110
Fulbright, J. William, 3, 6, 28, 65, 79, 107, 116, 118
Full-text system, 170, 172; *see also*, FLITE

García, Carlos, 67
Garret, Stephen A., 101, 106, 110, 118, 152
Gasch, Oliver, 156
General Accounting Office (GAO), 64, 126–127
George Amendment, 105–107
George, Walter, 104–108
Gilbert, Amy M., 111
Gillette, Guy, 104–105
Glenn, John, 138, 144, 147
Glenn Substitute (to the Treaty Powers Resolution, 1978), 144–145, 147
Glennon, Michael, 148, 153, 156, 175

Goldwater, Barry, 136, 156
Great Britain (United Kingdom), 5, 50, 64, 87, 100
Greece, 78
Griswold, Erwin, 93
Guatemala, 57, 60, 77
Gulf of Tonkin Resolution, 119, 162

Haiti, 78
Hansen, George V., 159
Health agreements, 11–12, 126
Helsinki Accord, 72–73
Hendrickson, Robert C., 108
Henkin, Louis, 28
Hill, Lester, 108
Hilsman, Roger, 56
Holmes, Oliver Wendell, 87–88, 94–95
Honduras, 60
Hopkins, Raymond, 127
Hughes, Charles Evans, 98
Hughes, Harold E., 75, 82
Hughes-Ryan Amendment, 75, 135
Hull-Litvinov-Agreement, 88, 99
Human rights, 89, 94–95, 98
Humphrey, Hubert H., 133, 163–164
Hyde, Charles, 98

Immigration and Naturalization Service v. Chadha, 155; *see also*, legislative veto
India, 104
Indonesia, 78
Industrial designs, 59
Information Systems Office (Library of Congress), 165
Inouye, Daniel K., 136
Institutional revolution, 120; *see also*, neo-insurgents
Intelligence Accountability Act (1980), 135–137
Intelligence agreements, 73–78, 126, 161
Interagency coordination, 127–128; *see also*, agency-to-agency agreements
Interdependence, 15
International Agreement Consultation Resolution (1978), 145–147
International Agreements File, 167
International Atomic Energy Board, 59
International Court of Justice, 117

203

Index

Iran, 57, 61, 78
Israel, 72, 155, 161, 174
Italy, 50, 60, 78

Jackson, Henry, 71, 108
Japan, 50, 60, 68
Jefferson, Thomas, 6, 75–76, 149
Johnson, Louis, 174
Johnson, Lyndon Baines, 15, 17, 20–21, 22, 25, 33–35, 39, 43, 45, 59, 61, 118–120
Jordan, Hamilton, 141

Katzenbach, Nicholas, 152
Kennedy, John F., 14, 15, 17, 20, 22, 25, 34–35, 39, 43, 45, 59
Kent, Sherman, 73
Khoman, Thanat, 63
Kirkpatrick, Jeane J., 52–53
Kissinger, Henry, vii, 53, 71
Kiwanis International, 93
Knappen, Marshall M., 112
Knowland Amendment, 101–102, 105, 152
Knowland, William F., 101, 103, 108, 118, 152
Koenig, Louis W., 109
Kuchenbecker, David J., 29, 124, 127, 152, 153, 173

Laos, 68, 77
Latin America, 44–48, 54, 100, 120, 178–179
League of Women Voters, 92
Leaks, 123
Lebanon, 61
Legislative oversight, 165, 173–174
Legislative veto, 135, 137, 139, 154, 173
Leigh, Monroe, 128
Liberia, 60, 176
Library of Congress, 128, 165
Libya, 61
Lincoln, Abraham, 57
Lippmann, Walter, 104
Long, Russell B., 115

McCarran, Pat, 109
McGovern, George, 116, 117
Madison, James, vii

Magnuson, Warren G., 108
Magsaysay, Ramón, 67
Marcos, Ferdinand E., 80
Mexico, 50, 59
Middle East, 44–48, 162, 163, 179
Migratory Bird Treaty Act (1918), 87
Military agreements, 10, 15, 17–18, 20, 23, 25, 36–39, 51, 57–63, 77–78, 80, 126, 137–139, 140
Military Assistance Program (MAP), 63
Military bases, 60, 64–65, 67, 69, 80, 140
Millikin, Eugene D., 108
Missouri v. Holland, 87–88, 94–96
Moore, John Bassett, 113
Morgan, Thomas, 138
Morgan-Zablocki Amendment (1975), 139, 147, 148
Moynihan, Daniel Patrick, 136
Murray, Mrs. Robert, 112, 117

Nash, Frank, 92
National Commitments Resolution (1969), 120; *see also*, 139
National Science Foundation, 129
National Security Act (1947), 76
National Security Affairs, Assistant to the President for, 129
National Security Council, 76
Nelson-Bingham Amendment (1974), 137–138
Nelson, Gaylord, 137
Neo-insurgents, 117, 151
Neo-isolationists, 116
New Deal, 90
Nixon, Richard M., 15, 17, 23, 24–25, 33–36, 39, 42–43, 45, 47, 59, 70–71, 72, 120, 121, 160
North Atlantic Treaty Organization (NATO), 49, 60, 69–70, 117, 161
North Korea, 77
Nuclear Regulatory Commission, 129
Nuclear Test Ban Treaty (1963), 60, 161
Nye, Joseph S., Jr., 127

Office of Legal Adviser for Treaty Affairs (Department of State), 8, 9, 124, 125–126, 128, 133, 143, 150, 162, 172
Office of Technology Assessment, 151

Index

Oral "understandings," 68, 126, 130–131, 161, 162
Orwell, George, 31

Pakistan, 50, 57, 61
Panama Canal Treaties (1977), 28, 141, 150
Paramilitary agreements, 76, 78
Paris Accord (1973), 70–71
Passport agreements, 11–12
Peru, 50
Philippines, 50, 57, 60, 66–67, 78
Point Four Program, 17
Pointing system, 170, 172; see also, SCORPIO
Poland, 77
Polar bears, 59
"Political" agreements, 72, 113
Portugal, 70
Potsdam, 91, 99
Power of the purse, 141, 148–149
Presidential power, 4, 57, 68, 71, 74, 79, 87, 100–101, 103, 106–107, 109, 118, 141, 150
Public opinion, 159–160
Punta del Esta Summit Conference, 119

Reagan, Ronald, 80
Rehm, John B., 58, 155
Reporting requirements (Statutory), 121, 126, 130, 143, 150, 163, 165–166, 169, 173, 184–186
  prior notification, 132–133, 135–136, 171
  consultation, 135, 137, 145, 160–161, 185
Republican Party, 86, 90, 103, 109, 114
Roosevelt, Franklin D., 5, 17, 90, 92
Rovine, Arthur W., 152, 153
Rush, Kenneth, 127–128
Rush-Bagot Agreement, 99–100
Rusk, Dean, 63–64, 69
Russell, Richard B., 78
Russia, 88
Ryan, Leo J., 75, 82

Saltonstall, Leverett, 65, 105–106
Saudi Arabia, 138

Schlesinger, Arthur M., Jr., 27
Schlesinger, James, 153
Schollaert, James T., 149
Schubert, Glendon A., 110, 111
Schweppe, Alfred, J., 96
SCORPIO (subject-content-oriented retriever for processing information online), 165–172
Secret agreements, 6, 20, 28, 63–64, 67–68, 70–71, 73–79, 90–91, 121, 125–126, 132, 136, 153, 161, 162, 168–169
Self-executing agreements, 95
Sinai Agreements, 71–72, 161–162
Sinai Support Mission, 71–72
Smithsonian Institution, 127
South Korea, 50, 57, 60, 67–68, 126–127
Southeast Asia Treaty Organization (SEATO), 63
Soviet Union, 36, 53, 71–72, 81, 88, 90
Spain, 64–66, 120, 141
Sparkman, John, 129, 145, 151, 171, 184–186
Special Trade Representative, 129
Spellman, Gladys, 138
Stassen, Harold, 92
States' rights, 87–91, 95–96, 106, 108, 118
Statutory agreements, 7, 8, 9, 12, 19, 40–42, 46–48, 51, 92, 100, 121
Stennis, John, 78–79
Strategic Arms Limitations Talks (SALT), 28, 29, 71, 141, 185
Surkarno, "Bungkarno," 78
Supreme Court, 87–89, 95, 97, 137, 155, 156, 173
Sutherland, Arthur E., 110, 113
Symington Subcommittee, 63–68, 120

Thailand, 63
Thieu, Nguyen Van, 71
Third-party agreements, 69
Tibet, 77
Tito, Josip B., 53
Totalitatian regimes, 32–36, 39–41, 53
Trade Act (1975), 137
Trade Expansion Act of 1962, 15
Transportation agreements, 11–12, 18, 25, 36–39, 51

Index

Treaties, 7, 8, 12, 19, 24, 40–42, 46–48, 51, 87–88, 97–98, 100, 140–141, 163
military treaties, 59, 62
Treaty powers, 3–4, 6, 28–29, 64, 66, 72, 79, 86, 93, 95, 97, 99–100, 113, 127, 140, 143, 146–148, 162
Treaty Powers (Clark) Resolution (1976), 140–145, 148, 150, 159, 181–183
Trujillo, Rafael Leonidas, 77
Truman, Harry S., 14, 15, 17, 21, 25, 33–35, 45, 47, 59, 133
Turkey, 50, 57, 61, 81
Tuttle, Elbert P., 112
Twenty-Second Amendment, 109, 115

Ukraine, 76
United Nations, 89–90, 92, 94–95, 102, 109
U.S. Air Force, 170, 172
U.S. Armed Services Committees, 65
U.S. Department of Commerce, 124, 129
U.S. Department of Defense, 70, 124, 126–128, 129, 170–171
U.S. Department of Health and Human Resources, 124
U.S. Department of Interior, 127
U.S. Department of Justice, 129
U.S. Department of State, 29–30, 66–68, 72, 77, 90, 97, 104–105, 121, 124–128, 129–130, 147–149, 151, 166, 169, 171, 174–175, 184–186
U.S. Department of Transportation, 129
U.S. Department of Treasury, 129
U.S. Government Printing Office, 172
U.S. House Foreign Affairs Committee, 121, 132, 134, 137, 138, 148–149, 164–165, 167–168, 172
U.S. House Intelligence Committee (Permanent Select), 126, 136–137, 172
U.S. Office of Management and Budget (OMB), 129
U.S. Postal Service, 129
U.S. Senate Appropriations Committee, 65

U.S. Senate Foreign Relations Committee, 6, 56, 65, 72, 91, 118–120, 121, 122, 123, 129–133, 140–145, 148, 164–165, 167–168, 172, 184–186
U.S. Senate Intelligence Committee (Select), 136, 172
U.S. Senate Judiciary Committee, 91–93, 109, 126
U.S. Senate Separation of Powers Subcommittee, 119
U.S. v. Pink, 87–89, 99, 110

Vance, Cyrus, 154, 163
Vandenberg, Arthur H., 90, 132–133
Veterans of Foreign Wars, 93
Vietnam, 63, 67–68, 71, 77, 161
Vietnam War, 85, 118–121
Vigilant Women for the Bricker Amendment, 93, 102
Vinson, Carl, 173

Wallace, Robert, 75
Warnke, Paul C., 81
Washington, George, 148
Watergate, 151
West Germany, 50, 60, 78
Western Europe, 44–48, 54, 60, 72, 178–179
Wheeler, Earle, 65
"Which clause" (Bricker Amendment), 96–97, 102–103, 105–106
White, William S., 113, 114
Wiley, Alexander, 91, 104
Wilson, Woodrow, 148
World government, 94, 109, 117

Yalta, 91, 99
Yugoslavia, 36, 53

Zablocki, Clement, 121; *see also,* Case-Zablocki Amendment and the Morgan-Zablocki Amendment